Gray Maxwell

Lays of the Dragon Slayer

Gray Maxwell

Lays of the Dragon Slayer

ISBN/EAN: 9783337267278

Printed in Europe, USA, Canada, Australia, Japan

Cover: Foto ©ninafisch / pixelio.de

More available books at **www.hansebooks.com**

Lays of the Dragon Slayer

By

MAXWELL GRAY

LONDON
BLISS, SANDS AND FOSTER
1894

PREFACE

THOUGH more than ten years—half ten years again—have passed since these Lays were written, they seem to the writer now, as then, in spite of defects and crudities, touched with the subtle magic that distinguishes poetry, however faulty, from verse, however perfect.

It seemed a sin, that increased with years, to leave them to yellow unseen in their dark drawer; but not until now was leisure found to bring them to light. After all, to publish poetry is not an indictable offence, nor does the writer echo the pious aspiration of Walt Whitman—

"Let him who is without my poems be assassinated!"

PREFACE

The last of the seven lays, "The Niblung Woe," still remains in that rare library in the castle Hawthorne built out of sunset clouds, and pillared with solid gold of morning sunbeams, alongside of the unwritten cantos of the *Fairy Queen*, the untold *Canterbury Tales*, the end of *Christabel*, and the remainder of Keats' *Hyperion*. Thence it may one day descend to shelves of terrestrial growth, should this volume meet with success.

Carisbrooke, I.W., 1894.

CONTENTS

	PAGE
CHRIEMHILD'S DREAM	7
SIEGFRIED'S GLORY	33
THE WINNING OF BRUNHILD	81
THE FATAL GIFTS	107
THE STRIFE OF THE SISTER QUEENS	127
THE LINDEN LEAF	161

NOTE

THE *Nibelungen Lied* is known to the writer only by Carlyle's unpleasant and patronizing essay, and the synopsis in Vilmar's *Deutsche Literaturgeschichte*. The *Edda* was first seen after some of these Lays were completed.

The writer has not seen either Mr. William Morris's treatment of the Niblung myths, or Wagner's music-dramas on the same.

Two of the Preludes—those marked with an asterisk—appeared in "*Westminster Chimes and Other Poems*" (Kegan Paul, Trench & Co.), 1889.

Lay the First

CHRIEMHILD'S DREAM

PRELUDE

The Rhine

THIS is the Rhine, the haunted Rhine!
    The chastened glow of evening falls
    On emerald waves and craggy walls,
On the golden green of the bending vine,
    On the storied Rhine.

Athwart the cliffs the gold lights slide;
    They tremble along the shadowed stream,
    They fire with swiftly dying gleam
The little boats that slowly glide
    On the quiet tide.

Sweet it were to drift for ever
    Between the broad Rhine's towered walls,
    Above his jewelled water-halls,
Above strange things that glance and quiver
    Beneath the river.

Was the bark wrought by mortal hand?
    It is unsubstantial as a gleam,
    And we, the shapes of a formless dream,
Float shadowy, like a spirit band
    From faëry land.

What is the song, the wondrous song,
    That winds about the winding river,
    Winding about and changing ever,
Now sad with deep and deadly wrong,
    Now sweet and strong?

Is it the fairy's charmèd lay,
    That takes the fisher, home returning,
    And fills him with a nameless yearning
Till he follows entranced away, away
    From the light of day?

Is it a voice from the dim, dark Eld,
    That thrills the waters laid to sleep,
    That echoes along the castled steep,
How valiant men those towers held,
    In the dim, dark Eld?

Is it the cry of patriot blood,
    That hallows the wave from age to age
    Is it the shriek of robber rage,
That ever has stained the holy flood
    With alien blood?

The voice of legend old and dim,
   Of fairy revel and fairy feast?
   The cry of the fierce and tortured priest,
Or warrior's shout or monk's sweet hymn,
   By the river's brim?

Or the tale of the dragon-guarded gold,
   A hero's dower to a wrongèd bride,
   Wrung of heart and crushed in pride,
When into the sunless wave they rolled
   The fateful gold?

Are the weird mist-children dwelling there?
   Do they guard beneath the emerald floor
   The blood-stained treasure's mystic store,
Do they wait and watch with weapons bare
   In the magic glare?

The topmost cliffs are tipped with gold,
   The climbing forest's winding maze
   Is wrapped in amethystine haze,
Crimson lights are sunk and rolled
   In the waters cold.

A towered city is shining fair
   In the glowing eve, and a gold-green sky
   Looks down on the vineyards terraced high,
The boat glides on like a passing care,
   In the perfumed air.

I trow a maiden is gazing down
  In the balmy eve from her crag-built bower;
  And a hid knight sings at the trysted hour;
He clings to the rocks that perilous frown
  On the water brown.

The river spirit is floating dim
  In the shadowy folds of darkening cliffs,
  His trailed robe draws the passing skiffs,
He sings, as he brushes the water's brim,
  His mystical hymn.

Beware of the touch of his mantle's hem!
  If it but sweep the vessel's rim,
  We are caught in the fold of his raiment dim,
We are dazed by the light of the pale green gem
  In his diadem.

Now the last glance of passing day
  Reddens a turret, far and fair;
  Dimly seen on the rocky stair,
A peasant is climbing his homeward way
  In the shadows gray.

He hears the music, faint and strange,
  He crosses himself for fear, I ween,
  Looks up at the crags that over him lean;
Higher and higher they seem to range
  As the shadows change.

THE RHINE

Our bark was never of mortal mould—
    Over the water's silent tide,
    Swift and sure as thought, we glide
Into the shades that softly fold
        The waters cold.

Who with us in the viewless bark
    Will float and dream on the storied Rhine?
    Who will look for the magic shine
Of treasure deep in the hidden ark
        Of the waters dark?

LAY THE FIRST

Chriembild's Dream

I.

DREAMS hold the cradled babe in peace profound,
   Blend with the perfume of joy's earliest blooms;
This mortal life is folded and enwound
   By deeper, stronger life, whence awful glooms,
   The shades and semblances of mighty dooms,
Or the dim reflex of majestic deeds
   From that vague world whose shape so darkly looms
Upon us, cross our sleep; and he who heeds
With careful thought these shades, life's veilèd future reads.

II.

For while the infant plays the sisters spin;
   He sports unthinking in the shining sun,
And the grim Norns the fated web begin;
   His spirit blooms, his passions, one by one,
   Enkindle, and the mesh is ever spun
Around him. So he springs to manhood's grace:
   This way or that he proudly deems to run
The awful lists arrayed for life's stern race,
Nor recks upon his brow the dread Norns' secret trace.

III.

But when in silence of the shadowed night
    He lies in youth's deep slumber softly bound,
Like levin on his spirit's inner sight
    Strange scenes burst, and he looks as one astound,
    As some wise seër, held in magic swound,
Beholds the lifting of the awful veil,
    Hears the strong accents of a speech profound;
Nor knows, but dimly bodes, some coming bale,
And wakes with bristling hair and features wild
    and pale.

IV.

He wakes; nor heeds he in the morning's joy
    The things that froze his blood in midnight still,
Nor knows the Future on the dreaming boy
    Hath gazed, or that the shade of coming ill
    Or good hath wrought this deep and deadly chill;
Nor of the dream that wraps the troubled dream
    We call our life, nor of the bounds to will
The Norns must set us, does the glad youth deem:
There are who know, they know fate's source and
    life's high stream.—

V.

O thou, who broodest on the chaos dread
    Of cosmic life; who through their tangled maze
The homeless stars hast steered, and safely led
    This air-poised bark through world-storms and
    the blaze

Of dying planets; sleep her soft wing lays
Not on thee, O Unwearied, nor may dream
   Thee touch; all things show clear beneath the rays
Of thy dread glance; Eternal, thee we deem
Of life, fate, power, and love the source and end
     supreme;

VI.

And thou our rough-hewn, rudely-fashioned ends
   Dost exquisitely shape with perfect skill,
Thou the fierce passion that so lavish spends
   Its strength, all gently swayst beneath thy will;
   Even evil things and vile at last fulfil
Unwitting thy behest, and thou dost wring
   From darkness light, and ordered calm distil
From th' everlasting storm, and quiet bring
From fury, thou above all tumult reignest king!—

VII.

The boy wakes; but a shadow clouds his path,
   Erewhile so sunny, and a memory
Of awfulness, as of a high god's wrath
   Or high god's lofty love that gloriously
   Enfolds some mortal in divinity,
Until the hour of glory or of gloom
   Shall strike, and he behind the veil shall see
That, shadowless, which erst did vaguely loom;
Thus lives he, all unvexed by thought of coming
     doom.

VIII.

So with Chriemhild it fared, Chriemhild, the child
   Of Uta, sprung from the Burgundian line
Of princes, they who ruled with sceptre mild
   At Worms, the ancient city by the Rhine.
   Uta had seen, before his strength's decline,
Her king fall pallid in the clutch of death;
   Then strove she, lest in grief her soul should pine,
And gave herself to train, with loyal faith,
The girl and three fair boys who breathed her lost
     king's breath.

IX.

Now, on the threshold of life's flowery May,
   The maiden paused in dawning loveliness,
Unvexed by any shadow, night or day;
   And, as life in the cell, before the impress
   Of pollened anther in the light caress
The dainty flower-cup's honeyed beauty hides,
   Lies unawakened, so to bane or bless .
Lay unknown germs in her; as ocean tides
Unknowing seek the moon, she to her life's goal
     glides.

X.

The day was done; long shadows stilly fell
   Upon the broad breast of the mighty Rhine,
The forest slept as in a low-breathed spell,
   The peasant left the pruning of his vine,

More redly glowed the ruddy stems of pine,
The sun's last glories stained the towers tall
  And hoary ramparts, as with heavenly wine,
From woodlands far the wood-dove's plaintive call
Blent with the varied song of myriad minstrels small.

XI.

Upon the bastioned wall the princely maid
  Moved silent in the evening's chastened light,
No more she led the dance, no more she played
  With noble damsels, who, in flower-wreaths dight,
  Made merry sport from May-day morn till night.
Nor would she taste the scented, spiced May-wine,
  But gazed afar, as though her spirit's sight
Saw what on mortal eye-ball may not shine:
So in her castle fared the princess by the Rhine.

XII.

This Uta saw, and knew the maiden vexed
  By shadows; for the queen was skilled in lore,
Not earthly; mighty warriors, perplexed
  In dream or counsel, laid their thoughts before
  That woman sage, and she, to whom the door
Of hidden things had opened, gazed with eye
  Far-visioned, and the veils from mystery tore:
Thus heroes honoured her with reverence high
As one who dwelt above our frail mortality.

XIII.

Night fell apace; the May-day mirth was done,
  The silent world in silvery sheen lay dressed,
Deep slumber held the earth from sun to sun;
  But Chriemhild, oft with mystic dream oppressed,
  Started with parching lip and throbbing breast,
And ere the dawning streamed in liquid gold
  Through the strait casement, she from broken rest
Arose and saw the dewy day unfold;
And, later, to the queen her visions dim she told.

XIV.

"Methought," she said, "and twice I dreamed the same,
  Abroad in woods I fared in bloomy May,
And heard small birds sing, when a falcon came,
  Of noble plume, and in the flowery way
  He stood, and me with looks did mutely pray.
Then I, for that I greatly feared to tread
  That narrow path, lest I the hawk should slay,
My scarf waved, deeming that he would have fled,
But to my wrist he flew and perched, devoid of dread.

XV.

"At this I greatly loved the gallant fowl,
  And took him home, and from my own hand fed.
Jesses I broidered and a silken cowl,
  And set a perch for him beside my bed,

And him I found in hawk's art nobly bred;
Then nowhere joyed the bird save on my wrist,
   But whoso chid me pecked he that he bled,
And oftentimes the gentle bird I kissed,
Nor would he meat or drink if I his feeding missed.

XVI.

"All this I dreamed; but more remains behind,
   So dim, so wondrous, as no speech may tell;
Meseemed one day my falcon in the wind
   Was hovering, and I watched in joy, so well
   The hawk poised; when two eagles fierce and fell
I saw above my gentle tercelet soar;
   I cried; but as he flew upon the swell
Of wind to me, the eagles swooped and bore
My bird to earth, and him with crooked beaks
      fiercely tore.

XVII.

"They tore my gallant hawk before my eyes,
   Nor could I hinder them that they him ate,
And then with bloody beaks I saw them rise
   On kingly plumes; and deep and deadly hate
   Burnt in me when those fierce birds soared elate,
While I was left to weep my falcon slain.
   And them long while in ambush did I wait
With archers, till I slew those birds; and stain
Of blood fell on me; then I waked in dread and pain."

XVIII.

Thus, with wide eyes and quivering nostril fine,
  The princess spake, yet all to tell forebore.
And Uta, "Well may I that dream divine
  And glad am I to rede thee of my lore;
  The gallant falcon that the eagles tore
Is some great hero, who thy love shall gain
  And, in such bliss as mortal not before
Hath known, shalt thou with him the golden chain
Of love wear; but at last thy hero shall be slain.

XIX.

"For all beneath the moon must have an end;
  Yea, this wide frame of earth and stars and sun
Shall like a shadow pass. But God thee lend
  His mercy, that thy husband be not done
  To death in youth!" Then Chriemhild stood as one
Astonished, and her tresses' wavy gold
  Shone in the vaulted chamber's twilight dim;
And the queen marvelled at the graceful mould
Of her whose burgeoned bloom but promised to unfold.

XX.

And there, as Chriemhild stood, the window pane,
  With deeds of ancient warriors blazoned fair,
Let the May sunshine fall in rosy stain
  Upon her clasped white hands and shining hair.

Then turned she shuddering from the crimson glare
And moved towards the arras; then again
 Returned, and stood before the carven chair
Of Uta—then she spoke, with light disdain
Thrilling her voice that marked her soul of noble strain.

XXI.

"And speakest thou of hero's love to me?
 Nay, mother, never shall Chriemhild resign
Her maiden freedom, and the dignity
 Of self-reliant joy to waste and pine
For man's love; never hero shall be mine,
Though moulded as a god, perfection's star,
 Though passing all the lordly lofty line
Of our divine forefathers; for great war
With loving comes, and woe and death love's music mar."

XXII.

Then Uta, wise with years, looked down and smiled,
 As those who know. "Be not too sure," she said;
"If thou wilt drink of joy's full cup, fair child,
 Man's love alone can fill it. Thou shalt wed
A mighty hero; thus shalt thou be fed
With bliss. Thou knowest not the strength and stay
 Of a good, great man's love; Heaven's mercy shed
This blessing on our frail and suffering clay;
Thy weakness know'st thou not, or life's thorn-tangled way."

XXIII.

Full softly sighed the widowed queen and wan,
  Musing her own love's early darkened beam :
" Fair daughter, ever since the world began,
  This is the minstrel's dearest, sweetest theme,
  This love which shadows forth, as some clear stream
A tower, Christ's loftier love to his fair bride ;
  But of its sweetness only those may deem
Who once the mighty spell have fitly tried,
And who once tastes of love all solace scorns beside.

XXIV.

" Why are we soft and fragile, prone to fears,
  Why pine our spirits frail for love and care,
How in the deathful dance of levelled spears,
  When the hoarse raven's banquet taints the air,
  How in the single sword-fight should we fare,
How, in the dark, deep forest's tangled maze,
  The lean wolf's spring, or fierce boar's fury dare?
In counsel, love, and solace lies our praise,
And much we need man's care and strength through life's rough ways."

XXV.

Then a swift lightning lit the azure mild
  Of Chriemhild's eyes, and quickly she replied,
" Methinks the spirit of my father's child
  Might meet the surge of battle's roaring tide,

Or face the grim beast in the forest wide;
But let that pass. A maiden's dignity
In deep seclusion dwells. And never bride
Of hero or of king shall Chriemhild be;
Youth's primal joy would I keep pure and sorrow-
free.

XXVI.

"Fair mother, never yet was wife or maid
Her soul that yold to sweet, seductive spell
Of love, but she with anguish trebly paid
The brief, bright bliss that to her portion fell.
Oft have I heard old wives at twilight tell
Of gentle maiden loved and left forlorn,
And minstrels sweetest sing when most they dwell
On bleeding hearts pierced through by love's sharp
thorn;
Thus, in the lighted hall, they sing how lovers
mourn."

SONG.

"Oh! why so blythe, sweet ladye,
When the white snow folds the lea,
Where the long, black night lies brooding,
And the blast howls angrily?"

"Oh! how should I be sighing,
When my true knight rides to me
Through the bitter blast's fierce howling,
Where the white snow folds the lea?"

"Ah ! why so sad, sweet ladye,
　　When the May is beaming bright
　And the merry May-dance whirling
　　And the May-meads lapped in light?"

"Ah ! how should I be laughing,
　　When my love lies cold and white,
　No might in the hero's sword-arm,
　　In his starry eyes no light?"

XXVII.

" Hark to my brother in the court below,
　While merry birds are singing sweet of May,
He sings of love, and love repaid by woe ;
　God guard the lad from love for many a day !
　Sweet mother, I with thee will ever stay,
With thee and my young brothers will I dwell ;
　So shall my life untroubled have its way,
Like some full-flowing stream majestic swell ;
Or in yon abbey gray find me a quiet cell.

XXVIII.

" There will I read old tales, by dead men told,
　And wear away long nights in musings high ;
For heaven to maiden vigils doth unfold
　The secrets oft of our humanity :
　There on the abbey terraces, that lie
Above the kingly river's emerald tide,
　The virtue hid of root and herb will I
Discover, and sick folk from far and wide
Will heal ; and many an art and joy make known
　　beside.

XXIX.

"But liever in this ancient hall of kings
  With thee and with my brethren I would be;
Then oft some holy priest of lofty things
  Might reason; then sick, poor folk I might see
  And solace; and with maidens, sorrow-free,
Abroad in spring through greenwood alleys fare
  With hawk and hound, or in a boat with thee
Adown the river float in summer air,
And tend sweet flowers and birds and bees, and
    have no care.

XXX.

"And, when grim winter with his tempests keen
  And icy fangs begins to rudely chide,
With dance and minstrelsy"—But here the queen
  Checked the fair princess in her joyous tide
  Of day-dream, and full tenderly replied,
"And wilt thou have thy heart untouched by care?
  Poor maiden! Gold in flame is purified,
High God through sorrow makes man's spirit fair,
And thou of woe's fierce flame must have thy fated
    share.

XXXI.

"Yea, thou must sorrow and thou must rejoice
  Beyond the common; for thy heart beats strong
Beyond the common; and to man the choice
  Is not. Yet in thine anguish let no wrong

Thee conquer; not as slaves who bear the thong
And scourge, bear thou the loving wrath of heaven;
  Who nobly sorrows will not sorrow long.
God grant man's treachery be never given
As poison in thy cup, nor bonds of blood be riven!"

XXXII.

Here Uta crossed herself and turned in haste
  And spoke more cheerily. "But not with woe
Would I thee sadden; deep joy shalt thou taste,
  Yea, with love's bliss thy cup shall overflow.
  Oh! bitter is her lot who walks below
On this bleak earth alone; what shield hath she
  From rudest blasts of scorn? Well doth she know
The hard, cold, pitiless world's scant charity,
Knows well that for the weak there is no liberty.

XXXIII.

"Yea, like a fair rose in a dungeon's night,
  Her beauty wastes, her sweetness is not known;
Well to a cloister may she take her flight,
  And hide in mighty arms of loveless stone.
  Dreary it is to sit at night alone
And muse by crackling pine-logs, or to gaze
  Through lattice bars upon the blue void strown
With holy watchfires; drear to hear the lays
Of mated birds, and walk green woods and flowery
    ways.

XXXIV.

" Dreary it is to feel high powers waste
  In dark oblivion, like brave fruits that rot
Untasted ; for, if we not by men are braced
  And strengthened, very darksome were their lot
  Without us ; who should curb the rash and hot
Intemperance of their blood, who soothe their pain,
  Who plant for them a green and gracious spot
In life's dry desert, who with silken chain
Of purer, gentler thought their world-worn spirits
    rein ?

XXXV.

" For when high God eternal would create
  The crown of all his creatures, not alone
One made he them, but twain, each with his mate,
  Before divine breath in our clay was blown ;
  Of other each is part, as bone of bone.
And know, fair child, before the babe's first cry
  The flower of woman's soul is still unknown,
Till she gives life she lives not quite, though high
Her soul's aim ; for her best locked in her heart
    must lie.

XXXVI.

" Wilt never hear the voices silvery sweet
  Of little clinging children cry to thee?
Like some half builded temple, incomplete,
  Unconsecrate by mysteries high, wilt be?

Or rather, like some fair and fruitful tree
Wide-branching, yield refreshing food and shade,
   That living creatures bless thy charity,
That in thy boughs full-brooded nests are made,
And at thy roots young lambs in noontide heats
     are laid?"

XXXVII.

Now, Chriemhild by a pillar stood inclined
   Before the queen, and at her knee a hound
Crouched fawning; him she stroked with absent
     mind,
   And ever in her ear the low, sweet sound,
   Like music touched by harper's skilful hand,
Of singing from the court an echo found,
   To Uta's voice. And deep in musings bound
She paused, as she would seek to understand
Themes that were tangled fast in mystery's shadowy
     band.

XXXVIII.

Deep-hearted Uta watched the dreamy haze
   Shadow the summer sunlight of her eyes,
And deemed, and rightly deemed, that on her gaze
   Life opened in new forms that did surprise
   And charm and terrify; as one that tries
A never-mounted steed, so, in her mind,
   The princess visioned yet unvisioned ties,
And felt strange joys about her heart-strings wind,
Then moved, as she some spell of magic would
     unbind.

XXXIX.

She moved, upon her lips a swift smile fled,
  The shadows left her sweet eyes, dewy blue,
A little loftier held her gold-bound head,
  And turned, like bird impatient of his mew;
" Fair Mother, wise are all thy words and true ;
But every creature doeth like his kind ;
  Stags roam by day, but wolves when falls the dew
From starry skies ; I would be unconfined
By love-bands, and alone and strong down life's
    vale wind.

XL.

" For I am not, as many a gentle maid
  I know, slight-built, a soft and fragile thing ;
Freedom I love ; I am not soon afraid ;
  Then why should I about a hero cling,
  As others use ? For bards of old time sing
Of might not earthly, given to maidenhood,
  That on the marriage morn takes instant wing ;
Old sagas tell of choosers of the dead,
Strong maids, and Valas wise, who in the future
    read :

XLI.

"And how are they beyond all women blest,
  Those virgins pure who live in convent cell !
Hath ever wedded wife such joys confessed
  As they of vision high and vigil tell?

And why should maidens lone and useless dwell?
Who better may the wounded warrior tend,
　Or gather orphans in the gentle spell
Of charity, who long night-watches spend
So well in searchings deep of things that cannot
　　end?

XLII.

"Yet rather I unfettered would abide
　Without the cloister; for I love the sun
And bright, blithe things, and would not darkly
　　glide,
　Like hidden stream, among the shadows dun;
But, like some mountain beck, rejoicing run
And leap with singing over crag and moss
　In sunlight. Now, sweet mother, I have done;
The morning ages, and the lindens toss
Their arms in joy, and shake their new robes' silken
　　gloss.

XLIII.

"Come out, and joy thee in the merry May
　Before it fades." Then rose the widowed queen,
And, set on palfreys fair, they took their way
　Down from the hoary burg through alleys green.
　And many a courtly dame, in satin sheen,
And fair-haired page, silk-suited, swelled their train,
　With maidens, brighter than the sunny scene
Around them. Thus with dance and minstrel strain
They filled the woods till eve blushed out in blood-
　　red stain.

CHRIEMHILD'S DREAM

SONG.

Play on, play on
  In the merry May,
Though the sisters are spinning
  By night and by day.

Sing on, sing on,
  While the world is young,
Ere the dark hour strike
  On the iron tongue.

Laugh on, laugh on,
  While laugh you may;
The swift hours are snatching
  Sweet youth away.

Dance on, dance on
  In the shining spring,
Nor dream in the mad whirls
  What winter may bring.

Laugh on, laugh on,
  While the earth is so fair,
Ere the soft-blowing woodlands
  Are leafless and bare.

Sing on, sing on;
  Over flower-bound brows
Glooms the weird sisters' spinning
  By mystical boughs.

LAY THE SECOND

SIEGFRIED'S GLORY

II.

PRELUDE

The Forest*

OH, let us pierce the billowy gloom
   That greenly wraps the mountain-side,
The woodland, clothing crest and coombe
With beauty. There white lilies bloom,
   Silk-sheathed, beneath oak branches wide,
     Where sunlights slide.

A stag down yon green vista fleets,
   A thousand joyous insects hum;
High up the leafy archway meets,
Tall lindens dream of summer sweets;
   On deep-mossed pathways footfalls come,
     All hushed and dumb.

Sweet woodruff breaks in balmy snow
   Beneath the columned aisles of beech,
Whose shining leaves the sunlight throw
In dimmed and broken shafts below,
   I hear the nuthatch tap his breach,
     And the cuckoo's speech.

Oh, the life and the joy of the gay greenwood,
  The glad live things that glance and play,
The song that falls in a silvery flood,
The beast in his lair and the bird with her brood,
  The bees, and the blossoms that light the way
    In the greenwood gay !

Beneath this mighty oaken dome,
  Where gnarled boughs gather a hoary gloom,
By silvery birch and prickly holm,
Beneath the princely beeches, roam
  To a glade where the light fern lifts his plume
    And the whitethorns bloom,

Roam on, and leave the weary world,
  And all its striving, all its care ;
Look down on the wave that is gently swirled
By the linden roots, all mossed and pearled
  With wet ; look back at the vaultings fair
    The beech-shafts bear.

Here belike, in the olden time,
  Some maiden, bound in a dim, dread spell,
Sat spinning in beauty beneath the lime,
When she heard the hunter's music chime,
  And the fair prince saw her beside the well,
    And loosed her spell.

THE FOREST

Sweet is the glade with shade and sun
   And the quiet speech of wave and wind ;
'T is sweet, the sands of noontide run,
To pace the pine-wood's cloister dun,
   Whose red-ribbed vaults of branches twined
      To sun are blind.

This is the fane of the dim Unseen,
   Of hidden powers high and vast ;
An awful stillness breathes serene,
Though deep-toned chants roll up between,
   As the black roof sighs to the long-drawn blast
      That is sweeping past.

A grey light gleams beyond the pines,
   Where a torrent roars by a rock-built tower,
Then gloom anew the lofty lines
Of pillared stems ; the day declines ;
   And now the sprites of the wood have power
      At the glooming hour.

The pine-wood breaks ; a crimson sun
   Fires all the rugged mountain walls.
What treasure rests in the caverns dun,
Deep where the day has never shone ;
   What jewels gleam in the echoing halls,
      Where no foot falls.

Far beneath, the elfin guard,
  Low of stature, swart of limb,
With glittering eyes keep watch and ward;
Woe to him who, evil-starred,
  Meets them in their caverns dim,
    Those watchers grim!

And woe to whom by sweet moonlight
  The water-spirits' revel breaks,
Or sees the strange and lovely sight
Of dancing elves and gnomes by night;
  If the elfin song his spirit takes
    No more he wakes.

It is an eerie thing by night
  To pace the forest's long arcades,
Where myriad things beyond the sight
Move darkling, where the moon gleams white
  In doubtful shapes on distant glades,
    Beyond the shades.

The glow-worm's lantern greenly beams,
  And white stars pierce the opening roof;
Come cheerly on, though the world of dreams
Breathes heavily round, and the wolf's eye gleams
  From under the covert's leafy woof,
    Where he watches aloof;

THE FOREST

Come cheerly on! Deep, deep below
   The forest slopes dark to the river's brim.
But yonder I see a ruddy glow;
Are they dwarfs or gnomes, whose shadows go,
Fitful and wild in the firelight dim,
      Are they spectres grim?

Nor gnome nor sprite, but of mortal mould,
   They move by the charcoal-burner's fire;
Rough hands, warm hearts, and spirits bold,
Their bitter sweat for scant bread sold;
   Here is their hut with its little byre
      By the dark fir spire.

Here we may rest in the fitful glow,
   Couched king-like on sweet boughs of pine,
And watch the weird, wild lustre show
Black sprays above, red stems below,
   While we pledge our host in the country wine,
      And the sweet stars shine.

The red light plays on his wind-beat face,
   While he tells his legend and sings his song.
On a sudden he stops for a little space,
And crosses himself, as a sound of grace,
   A chapel bell, steals sweet along
      The vaulting strong.

Nor sprite, nor fay, nor kobold grim
  Hath power while the sweet bell rings;
Birds sleep upon the great oak's limb,
Beasts prowl among the shadows dim;
  Now slumber sinks with folded wings
    Till morning springs.

What dreams will hold the sleepers' souls,
  The sleepers breathing balmy pine?
The forest's murmur round them rolls,
The stars sweep on in glittering shoals,
  The night-wind whispers thoughts divine
    In music fine.

LAY THE SECOND

Siegfried's Glory

I.

HE stood against the newly-risen sun,
    Before his father's gates; a golden haze,
Like to a regal vesture, featly spun
    And richly broidered in a wandering maze
    Of leaf and flower, of bright and broken rays,
Swept round his lofty form's heroic mould;
    Godlike he stood, his armour made a blaze
Red-glowing in the sun's fresh-burnished gold,
His shield and spear and sword, rich-jewelled, glittered cold;

II.

Upon his lip young manhood's early bloom
    Lay lightly, his blue eyes were dewy clear;
The crest that clasped his helmet's floating plume
    A flying dragon seemed, and all his gear
    Was bossed or graven with this shape of fear,
So that all men, beholding, Siegfried knew,
    Siegfried, the child of Sigmund, who with spear
And sword, undreading, the fierce dragon slew,
And from the secret caves the guarded treasure drew.

III.

Thus stood he smiling in the new-rayed sun ;
    Around him grouped his men, a gallant train.
With treasure laden, by his prowess won,
    And Sigmund's gifts, robes richly dyed in grain,
    Armour and gems and ruddy gold—bright bane
Of human hearts—a score of waggons rolled.
    Queen Siegelind to keep the lad was fain,
Full sore she wept and straitly did enfold
Her glorious son in arms that could not loose their hold.

IV.

And all who dwelt within the princely hall
    At Santen, built beside the unresting Rhine,
Had issued forth, and by the towers tall
    Stood gazing in the morning's early shine ;
    And many an eager soul did inly pine
To follow Siegfried on his knightly quest,
    To drink with him of peril's quickening wine,
And bright fame pluck from battle's horrent crest;
But Sigmund spake of fears within his boding breast.

V.

" Sore I misdoubt me, fair and noble son,"
    He said, "if this thy quest may bring thee good ;
Unboding, ere thy glory had begun
    Or thy bright blade yet drunk of any blood,

As a man lifts a noble falcon's hood
And shows the quarry, did I bid thee go,
  When, like the unblossomed rose, in silken snood
Deep-folded, thy great powers far below
Thine outward seeming lay in lustre soon to glow.

VI.

" I saw thee go, I saw thee come again
  With joy; I sent thee empty from my side,
In tenderest youth, unproven, with no rein
  To curb thee, save thy young will purified
    By prayer. And soon thou brought'st me bliss and pride
And sword-won treasure, O heroic son !
  But now thou goest, full of glory, tried
In peril, mightier than any one
Of woman born—yet I this quest for thee would shun.

VII.

" Thy mother weeps, with secret fears oppressed
  And omens, such as gloom on wifely soul
Unstained ; and could we hold thee from thy quest
  Nor spot thine honour, then were bitter dole
    Spared the warm hearts where kindled first the coal
Of thy bright life—yet it were better far
  To see thee lifeless, wrapped in bloody stole,
Than that vile ease or sloth thy fame should mar,
And thou from honour's heaven shouldst sweep, a fallen star."

VIII.

Then fair and courteously Prince Siegfried said,
  (His sunny face with hope and joy alight),
"Fair sire, sweet mother, on this quest is laid
  My honour; I have sworn on faith of knight
  To win the fairest, under heaven's bright
And starry round; and did I fail to try
  My fortune, knowing her ye ken in sight
Of all men fairest, then would red shame dye
My name—yet would I not woe on your hearts should lie.

IX.

"And wherefore dread ye? To the deathful dance
  Of crimsoned spears I go not, but in peace
To win the light of beauty's beamy glance
  In bloodless battle, and a maid release,
  Not from fire-breathing dragon, but the ease
Of white, unwakened, maiden fantasy;
  Ye know me strong in fight, I pray you cease
Your grieving, speed my parting cheerily,
And bless me that I go with spirit sorrow-free."

X.

He spoke and bowed him; on his sunny hair
  The fresh light played, and all around him shone.
The princely parents sped with words of prayer
  Their mighty child; the liegemen, one by one,

Bade farewell. Then, all words of parting done,
The hero leapt upon his armoured steed,
   And moving gleamed as sheathed in molten sun,
Smiled joyous farewell; then with easy speed
The cloud of shining spears waned slowly to a bead

XI.

And ceased. Within the hall the parents went,
   Musing on Siegfried's deeds and all his might,
But chiefly how the tidings first were sent
   Of Chriemhild's beauty. It was one wild night
   Of that tempestuous moon whose fitful light
Is kindled on the April side of Yule;
   The turrets shook with storm, the hall was bright
With flaming cresset, warm with glowing fuel,
Where men sat safe and heard the hurt winds wail
      and pule.

XII.

So fierce a night it was, the song and tale
   That oft beguile the warman's hearth were still;
The rugged music of the rattling hail,
   The war-god's arrows, and the wailings shrill
   Of baffled spirits wreaking their wild will
In tempest on the burg's embattled towers,
   Held the strong warriors' hearts with awe, until
A flash of green fire lit the sleety showers,
Gleamed in the hall and passed, and then the rolling
      powers

XIII.

Of Thor's deep thunder all the heavens broke,
  And Siegfried's men upstarted, unawares,
When a tall pinnacle beneath the stroke
    Fell crashing, so that men, in the swift glares
    Out-gazing from the pane with dazzled stares,
Saw the stone crumble in the court below;
  Then gathered the strong fury of the airs
And smote the oaken gates so fierce a blow,
The hasps and staples snapped, and slowly to and fro

XIV.

The heavy gates swung grating on the yard—
  All heard them in the lulling of the wind.
Then rose the Dragon-slayer and unbarred
    The hall door, gazing out if he might find
    Some foe, but all was lost in darkness blind.
Then forth into the gusty storm he fared,
  With many warriors following behind;
And each man in the dark his weapon bared,
And fierce, as if in fight, into the blackness glared.

XV.

Now when they reached the gate the moon outbroke
  In sudden glory from a fissured cloud,
And, as the youthful prince his challenge spoke,
    He saw the figure of an old man bowed

By years; a monk's gray garment his sole shroud
From storm; upon his white and reverend head
　The keen sleet drove and railed the tempest loud,
And forth-leapt blades fierce radiance on him shed;
Him the prince gently hailed, and through the
　　rough storm led.

XVI.

He led him to the warm and lighted hall,
　Nor spake the old man any word until
His robe was shaken from its snowy pall,
　Then, wet and wind-beat, pausing on the sill,
　He cried, "Goodwill to men of honest will!"
So, blessing, entered that great hall of kings.
　Then suddenly the roaring blast was still,
The wearied tempest folded his wild wings
And slept, like Furies charmed by Orpheus' golden
　　strings.

XVII.

All rose to do the old man reverence
　While the prince led him to the crackling pine,
And he, outglancing from the pent-house dense
　　And gray, that shadowed his deep-burning eyne,
　Marked well the stature tall and features fine
Of Siegfried, and he smiled a subtle smile;
　Spreading thin hands before the blaze—a sign
He made, low murmuring in his beard the while—
Then watched the hero move and speak in princely
　　style.

XVIII.

There lay a shadow on the lustrous brow
  Of Siegfried, and his eyes with brooding thought
Were darkened; for within his soul a vow
  Burned stilly and to high emprise him wrought;
  A fairy dream in golden mesh had caught
His springing manhood, and all things seemed stale
  And profitless until he should have brought
That lovely, lofty dream within the pale
Of breathing, warm-blood life, and raised its shadowy veil.

XIX.

And this sweet mystery his spirit took
  With longing past all speech. Long time the dream
Had stirred within the deep and crystal brook
  Of consciousness: when morning's youngest beam
  Touched the far, misty hills with rosy gleam,
His soul was haunted by a loveliness
  Beyond all thought; at evening still, supreme
It swayed him, till his longing's passionate stress
Wrought it to maiden semblance, tall, with floating tress

XX.

Of purest, beamiest gold; and deep, sweet eyes
  Held his, awake or sleeping, in rapt gaze,
With mystic power like that of winter skies,
  When large white stars flood all the trackless ways

And all night long in silent glory blaze:
Then in devotion to that lovely thing
　His strong soul bowed, and old heroic lays
Swept deeper, stronger, through the tuneful string
Of life, and all his thoughts soared up on mightier
　　wing.

XXI.

Till a most deadly weight of loneliness
　Crushed blank upon him ; then at times a sound
Of silvery speech his thrilling ear would bless ;
　Anon swift spells of deep emotion bound
　His soul and all his powers in magic wound ;
So in the silence of his secret breast
　The stir within a path to action found,
And Siegfried vowed to seek the loveliest
And win ; but never this to living wight confessed.

XXII.

Thus with the prince it fared, and thus his brow
　Was shadowed, and all present joys were vain.
In his soul's inmost cell he nursed the vow,
　Brooding on nobler deeds and vaster gain
　Of glory, till his glorious youth with pain
He viewed, as all unworthy in the light
　Of maiden glances ; for the instinctive strain
Of Nature lifts fair souls to summits bright,
Keen-aired and pure: thus seemed it in the stranger's
　　sight.

XXIII.

And ever held he in his burning gaze
    The Dragon-slayer, moving in the hall.
Now, while this old man rested by the blaze,
    The serving-folk brought meats, and set them all
    On tables in the light of torches tall
By warriors borne. And then with music came
    The king and queen; beneath a golden pall
They sat on high, enringed with knight and dame,
And bards to citherns sang brave deeds of olden
    fame.

XXIV.

Then flowed red wine and golden gleaming mead,
    And on the singers fell a fire divine:
Of ancient gods, who ruled before the creed
    Of Christ, the king, dark places made to shine,
    And of dim things that boded their decline,
Of Vala, Valkyr, of the dwellings fair
    Of gods, the mighty snake whose coils entwine
The world beneath that tree whose branches bear
All living things—they sang, and powers of earth
    and air;

XXV.

"Their glory and their strength have passed away,
    And fallen is every bright and awful throne,"
So sang, compassionate of vanished sway,
    Those bards in wild and wailful minor tone.

Then the old man his wanderings made known
From shrine to shrine in countries strange and far,
  Till every listening face seemed carven stone,
Nor dared men breathe, lest they his tale should mar;
His words in music rang like some deep-chiming
    star.

XXVI.

Yea, and the king and queen hung breathlessly
  Upon the strange charm of the old man's tongue;
Anon they asked themselves, "How may it be
  That he such music from the stars hath wrung?"
  The cressets flickered and the arras, hung
Around, waved all its broidered mimicry
  Of battle, chase, and lute by lover strung,
As stirred by airs divine. Then suddenly
He ceased, and all sprang up as from a spell
    set free.

XXVII.

Now when the feast was ended, and the queen
  And king withdrawn, all gathered in the glow
Of high-stacked logs, the while the guest, with mien
  Unchanged, spake on to all the listening row;
  He spake of beauty: "Many maids I know,
Fair, wise, and noble, but the fairest flower,
  The princeliest, the purest earth can show,
Blooms sweet and still in far, secluded bower
At Worms, where brethren three sway one united
    power."

XXVIII.

As when a spark leaps from a hunter's fire
  And, snatched by winds, is dropped on moorland brake
Sun-dried, the waste is wrapped in garment dire
  Of sudden flame, nor dew nor rain may slake,
  So fared the prince; he felt his bright dream wake
To breathing bloom, felt all the smouldering heat
  Within his bosom blaze, great yearnings take
His breathless soul in Love's strong spell and sweet;
Then mused he what high deed to win her would be meet.

XXIX.

And, as the vermeil deepens in the rose
  When the young day leaps through the flame-barred east,
Till crimson glory from its portal flows,
  Stirring warm nests and wakening bird and beast,
  So the firm red in Siegfried's face increased,
Hearing this ancient man of Chriemhild tell;
  And much he questioned; nor would he have ceased
But that the sage on other subjects fell,
Charming his listeners' hearts, he spake so wise and well.

XXX.

He spake so well, that all things heard him fain,
  Warman and serving-man and hawk and hound,
Even carved and painted men and flames, the chain
  Of eloquence so mightily enwound,
  That they warm sentient life a moment found;
And round the hoary sage with chime of bell
  The hawks, by dreaming falconer unbound,
Pressed closely; no one marked them in the spell,
And how the long night closed not one at morn could tell.

XXXI.

And of the stranger they no trace could find,
  But each man marvelled had he dreamed a dream;
His wild words seemed as when sleep's coils unwind
  From waking souls in morning's dewy beam,
  And they of fleeting glories vaguely deem,
Striving in vain to grasp the vanished clue
  Of arrowy joys, that pass with fitful gleam
Athwart the brain's dark chamber. These things threw
On Chriemhild's name a light of bale that daily grew.

XXXII.

But Siegfried held him closely to his oath
    And straight began his journey to prepare ;
Nor did his sire restrain though sorely loth
    To send him. Thus, when April's tender air
    Breathed sun and shower on field and forest bare,
And prisoned life burst forth in loveliness,
    And Nature, maid-like, blushed to find so fair
Her beauty in her fresh, flower-cinctured dress,
Forth fared he, deeply drawn by spring's life-giving
    stress.

Part II.

Siegfried's Glory

I.

IN the soft splendour of an April noon
    The travellers paused upon the Rhineland shore;
The first pale flush of summer's leafy boon
    Touched elm and hazelwood, white cloudlets bore
    Shadow and sunlight in their voyage o'er
A dim, deep sky, as full of mystery
    As olden Saga ; where oak branches hoar
Warm coppice hid, heart-stirring melody
Came flooding, liquid, pure and rich from blossomed
    tree ;

II.

The cuckoo called, the glancing swallow swept
    In airy curve, and hummed the roving bee;
In Siegfried's heart spring's mighty pulses leapt,
    Earth laughed with lustihood and jollity :
    Then a swart Niblung, from a lofty tree,
The kingly towers and spires of Worms descried,
    So fared they forward over blossomed lea,
And reached the castle by the river side
And paused in glittering ranks above the azure tide.

III.

Now the three kings beheld that bright array,
   From a high donjon, and they marvelled all,
Musing who might he be that held in sway
   Those warmen, Niblung swart and Teuton tall;
The armoured splendours and the golden pall
On laden wains, the gems, with wonderment
   They viewed, and deepest awe on them did fall
Of Siegfried's strength and beauty; and they sent
For Hagen, liegeman true, their wonder to content.

IV.

Von Troneck Hagen, who in many lands
   Had wandered, and all famous heroes knew,
All manners strange and tongues; he, their commands
   Receiving, swiftly came; long glanced he through
   The narrow casement; then deep breath he drew
And said, "All noble heroes have I known
   Save him who won the Niblung gold and slew
The dragon, and the sightless cloak alone
From Alberich tore; his fame from land to land is blown."

V.

Then spake he briefly of the glorious deeds
   Of Siegfried, ere his manhood's full-dawned morn;
How all alone, unvexed by dainty needs,
   He wandered, armoured fully by his scorn

Of evil, and all wights of succour lorn
He succoured, and from evil magic freed
  Much people, and, by noble yearnings borne,
Pressed on o'er barren hill and blossomed mead
Into a weird, wild wood and wrought his mightiest
    deed.

VI.

That forest gloomed beneath a blasted heath,
  Deep, dark, and sunless, chill as moulding tomb;
Siegfried, like one adream, drew from its sheath
    His shining sword, as if some evil doom
    He felt before him through the shadows loom;
And onward pressed beneath the mazes hoar
  Of thickly branching oaks in deepening gloom;
Those gray-haired kings the rose-beams never wore
From fresh Aurora's brow, or Dian's silvery ore;

VII.

Nor ever blaze of noon or star-beam fell
  Through the thick folding of that living roof,
No flower that loves the sun her dainty bell
    Swayed in the breeze, no blossom-braided woof
    Of moss, soft-spreading, dumbed the passing hoof;
A ragged undergrowth of tangled brush
  Strayed in fantastic shapes and held aloof
The band of princely trunks, and in the hush
Anon some evil beast made sudden stealthy rush.

VIII.

The hero made a lustre in the gloom,
    Like diamond dropped in beauty's raven hair,
And nowise paled his cheeks' young healthy bloom,
    His sunny curls illumed the dusky air,
    His drawn sword flashed with fitful lightning glare;
Firm and serene the tangled path he trod,
    Now baffled, like a bright bird in a snare,
Now smitten by the quick rebounding rod
Of ash or oak, now sunk in lush, marsh-nourished sod.

IX.

Only a strange oppression weighed his heart,
    And checked his strong breath in the heavy air;
Now glittering serpents on his path would dart,
    And now he roused a fierce beast from its lair;
    As moves a brave man, gnawed by myriad care,
With dreadless front and never-conquered will,
    So moved the undaunted prince; and now a stair,
Steep-breathed, the path seems, climbing sudden hill,
Here giant pines, deep-rooted, balmy scents distil.

X.

So fared he till he gained a heathery glade,
    High up, and heard afar a torrent roar;
Athwart the sandy waste his way he made,
    When a vast moving shadow loomed before,

And lo! a giant clad in wolf-skin bore
Upon him, whom the prince full gently hailed;
   Then the wild man, not bred in courteous lore,
The youth for answer with his staff assailed,
But Siegfried's sword leapt forth so swift, the giant quailed

XI.

And abjectly the prince's grace implored,
   That Siegfried granted with a light disdain;
Then spake the man of Niblung's golden hoard,
   Of damsel bound in rude oppression's chain,
   And him would guide across the wind-shorn plain.
So on they fared in converse, till the guide
   The youth unguarded found and smote again,
But the brave boy the huge beam dashed aside
And fought the giant fell and smote him that he died.

XII.

And then, forspent and worn with heavy strife,
   Down sank the prince upon his bossy shield,
Musing the words of him whose streaming life
   Made round his carcase huge a crimson field,
   When on the wind an anguished crying pealed,
Far borne; full swiftly then the hero rose
   And onward pressed in triple daring steeled,
Jagged steeps around in narrowing chasm did close
And mountains soared above him into gleaming snows.

XIII.

Below his feet a deep gorge darkly yawned,
   With forest clothed ; far down a river rolled ;
And lo ! a fearsome brood by demon spawned,
   Fire-breathing, sharp-winged, from the rocky hold
   Swarmed out and clanged around him; then four-fold
In agony, arose the cry again ;
   Well wist he then the mountain held the gold
Of Niblung far in darkly winding vein,
And he exulting smote the dragon swarm amain.

XIV.

The lofty joy that noble spirits feel
   On life's high summit, when their utmost might
Is tested, and, as stricken stone to steel,
   Long hidden fire they yield, whose sudden light
   Leaps up enkindling flames that quench the night,
Thrilled all the deeps of Siegfried's mighty soul ;
   And while he smote, more radiantly bright
His bright face grew ; but dark, despairing dole
Seized the gold guards, who felt earth's deep-sunk pillars roll.

XV.

They felt earth's pillars roll beneath the storm
   Of that fierce fight and trembled far within ;
Without, a cloud of fire enwrapped the form
   Of Siegfried, his fierce-smitten shield a din

Tremendous made; out of the mail-sheathed skin
Of those winged monsters hissing crimson poured,
  And some adown the gorge with rapid spin
Fell lifeless, till before that deadly sword
The whole fierce dragon swarm fled trembling,
    slashed and gored.

XVI.

Then Siegfried paused victorious, but his blood
  Flowed fast, though he not felt it in the glow;
Wiping his brand, he mused how he the flood
  Might cross, that boiled with giddy swirl below,
  And scale the rocky stronghold of his foe,
When the dim air grew black with hissing smoke
  And a long serpent sailed on pinion slow
Athwart the darkened sky; fire-torrents broke
From his deep-caverned eyes and wrapped him like
    a cloak.

XVII.

Now Siegfried's nostril quivered, and his breath
  Came chokingly, but he with steadfast gaze
Defiant looked upon that swooping death;
  His back against the rocky wall he stays,
  His good shield lifts against the blinding blaze,
His long spear plants; the dragon's hovering pause
  With torturing malice he long time delays,
  Until with sudden swoop the sharp crook'd claws
Clutch round the prince and flame him blinds from
    gaping jaws.

XVIII.

In giddy circle through the blasted air
    The dragon rose with his unconquered prey;
Then came a struggle fiercer than despair,
    Till Siegfried's keen-edged blade a secret way
    Beneath the jointed scales found; in dismay
And pain the monster lashed his barbèd tail
    And roared that shepherds heard him far away
By folded flocks; then through the hero's mail
His strong teeth crashed; with pain the boy's flushed
    cheek grew pale,

XIX.

And he had well-nigh swooned for agony,
    But that his strong heart rose in that fierce throe,
And in the dragon's throat so suddenly
    He thrust his sword, he made a great vein flow
    In the unarmoured flesh; with gurgles low
The monster's teeth and claws relaxed their hold,
    And for pure pain the noble prey let go;
In many a dizzy turn the hero rolled
Through sinking air, till prone he struck upon the
    mould,

XX.

And there bereft of consciousness he lay,
    Like crushed lamb dropped from stricken eagle's
        claw,
While the great wounded dragon in dismay
    Flew to his stronghold, pouring from his jaw

Hot flaming blood, until the fissure raw
He staunched; then forth he flew again with roar
    Far-pealing, and his vast tail like a saw
All jagged cut the air; his great vans tore
The clouds, as he above the lessening mountain bore.

XXI.

Now Siegfried on the farther side was dropped
    Of the dark torrent, swirling deep below,
And though awhile his great heart's pulses stopped
    For lack of blood and fury of his blow,
    Life's deep-laid current soon regained its flow
And he, awaking from his heavy swoon,
    Saw linden boughs sway gently to and fro,
And round his limbs he felt the grateful boon
Of deep-piled moss, and all his powers he gathered soon.

XXII.

Yet would he fain have rested for a space,
    Safe-hid in moss and fern, but that wild cry
Of maiden mewed in evil hiding place,
    Pealed out again in deepening agony;
    Then leapt he to his feet, resolved to die
At least in succour of that helpless one,
    And as he moved, he saw the monster, high
Outspread in air, enwreathed by vapour dun,
And felt exulting strength through all his pulses run.

XXIII.

So scents the steed the battle from afar,
  Shaking with joy his thunder-clothèd mane;
In fancy down the bloody ranks of war
  He flashes, and he treads the pallid slain
  With iron heel, as men the golden grain
For life's sustaining bruise; with shrilling cry
  He bounds exulting o'er the windy plain,
Nor recks he of the dreadful agony
Of screaming steed death-struck, so he in fight
    may be.

XXIV.

Siegfried betook him to a deep-niched cleft,
  By fire-throe ruptured in the living rock,
And scarce his gleaming blade in hand he heft
  Ere the fierce dragon pounced with stunning
    shock
  Upon him, safe immured in granite block;
And though the mountain shudders to its heart,
  And the swayed trees their crests together knock,
Siegfried is scathless; but the guardians swart
Of Niblung's golden hoard with bristling hair
    upstart.

XXV.

Dark clouds of smoke with fire commingled rolled
  So thickly, Siegfried scanty breathing found,
Like warriors in a city's central hold,
  When storming foes have scaled the ramparts
    bound,

And the strong citadel with flame surround;
But soon the baffled monster rose again
  On mighty wheel and measured all the ground,
Like a skilled captain who would lay his train
Beneath a stone-walled town and raze it to the plain.

XXVI.

Then Siegfried's pulses leapt and forth he came,
  Unsheltered in free air, with joyous cheer;
Where his foot smote, away rolled eddying flame,
  Like clouds that part in fire when morn leaps clear
Above the dark hill-tops; devoid of fear,
The hero saw with bright and steadfast eye
  The fiery creature through the air-waves steer,
Its gleaming armour lit with varied dye,
And, like Thor's wielded bolt, shoot thundering from the sky.

XXVII.

The prince's heart throbbed, yet he swervèd not,
  But met the monster with uplifted sword,
And, seeking carefully a jointed spot
  In th' armoured trunk, straight towards the vitals bored;
  A blinding flood about the smiter poured,
And the hurt monster with spasmodic clutch

The boy tight gripped and through his cuisses
    gored
And left him, but, before a second touch,
Siegfried his shelter reached and breathed, rejoicing
    much.

XXVIII.

Then frenzied fury seized that dragon fierce,
    And on the rock he beat with frantic blows
Wings, tail, and body; but he could not pierce
    Where Siegfried housed; so, under soft-piled
    snows
Unfrosted, some fair plant whose life stream flows
    Towards the spring, resists the icy blast
    That overhead in whirling tempest goes;
He stood, as he in sculptor's mould were cast,
To smite with all his strength one furious blow and
    last.

XXIX.

Then the swart watchers trembled far within,
    Feeling the quivers of the pillared mine,
They feared the mountain's falling in the din
    And rooting up, like tempest-smitten pine;
    So, whispering together, they combine
To bear the treasure forth before the crash
    Their blood should mingle with the jewels' shine;
The heavy ore upon their backs they lash,
Thus, in day's dying beam, red gold and diamonds
    flash.

XXX.

But Siegfried, all unwitting their dismay,
  Stood gathered for his fierce and final blow,
And smote at last so true and sure, its way
  His steel found to the vitals of his foe;
  Fierce writhed the dragon in his dying throe,
And stiffened all along the mountain side,
  And from his corse a fiery overflow
Of hissing blood poured out in mighty tide,
Most like the flaming wave that threads Hell's champain wide.

XXXI.

Then Siegfried rested in the ruddy glow
  Of eve, forspent and wounded by the fight;
In thankful joy he marked the overthrow
  Of the huge beast and marvelled at his might;
  Thus, stayed upon his sword, his features bright
And shining hair all marred with blood and smoke,
  In prayer lost, a swiftly kindling light
Like tropic sea-dawn o'er his visage broke,
When he the lady saw, unprisoned by his stroke.

XXXII.

Who was that lady? and what evil spell,
  By what enchantments forged, upon her lay?
What anguish tore her heart, in what dim cell?
  Of what dark tyranny was she the prey?

What to the prince did that sweet lady say,
Smiling before him in the sunset glow?
And whither wandered she at shut of day?
Bring back lost bloom of forty years ago,
But this from Hagen's lips let no man hope to know.

XXXIII.

Now, when that lady left him, in the tide
   Of hissing blood he plunged, of raiment spoiled;
Thus he endued himself on every side
   With viewless armour, as about him coiled
   The hot wave in the dragon's fierce heart boiled;
Thence issued he, as carved in marble white,
   All wounds healed, and as he had never toiled,
Of loftier stature and of greater might,
Unwoundable, and clothed in beauty manlier bright.

XXXIV.

But ere the bath, a fluttering lime-leaf fell
   Between his mighty shoulders, so that spot
Escaped the sheathing. Now the unseen shell
   So strong was that the steel is forgèd not,
   The beast unborn, unkindled yet the hot
Flame's breath of power to pierce it. Raiment
     brought
   The courtly dwarfs, bright-hued and fair, and got
Him armour, rich and curiously wrought
In the deep underworld by sun or star unsought.

XXXV.

And all the treasure of the Niblung hoard,
  Rich-hearted ruby, sardius, sapphire blue,
Silver and burning gold, long darkly stored,
  They piled in glowing heaps before his view;
  There flashed the diamond's drop of fiery dew,
The emerald's flame, the beryl's sea-tinged light,
  The opal's sweet and ever-changing hue,
The moon-rayed pearl; they made the gloaming bright,
Siegfried, beholding them, saw not the gathering night.

XXXVI.

But gazed with dim, fixed glance, as one by power
  Of glamour held. The sun was two hours gone,
Dead from the west fell day's last paling flower,
  Earth gloomed, woods drowsed, Heav'n's purple plains were strown
  With dewy stars, a young moon paced alone,
With virginal calm glance, the orient height,
  The hushed flood murmured low, a misty zone
Lay curling round the mountain, ghostly white,
When Siegfried saw an army moving through the night.

XXXVII.

They moved with noiseless footfall down the glen,
  The still air fluttered not their banners bright;
Prince Siegfried marvelled, were they living men,
  Or phantoms woven of the moonbeams white?

Up rose the dwarfs, all trembling at the sight,
Crying, "Niblung and Schilbung's hosts behold!"
Then in night's shadows raged a deadly fight,
And when the fresh dawn kissed the mountain cold
She touched a crownless king and conquered host
    with gold.

XXXVIII.

Thus Siegfried won the realm and golden store
    Of Niblung; many noble deeds beside
He wrought, remembered well in minstrel lore;
    The cloak of darkness, that from sight could hold
    Who wore it, he could all securely glide
Through throngs of armèd foes in summer noon,
    From the dwarf Alberich he tore, and, dyed
In darkness, things he wrought beneath the moon,
Whence glorious fame he reaped that will not
    moulder soon.

XXXIX.

This Hagen briefly told in quick rough speech,
    With rapid glances from his burning eyes.
Then mused the kings if it were churlish breach
    Of courtesy to close their gates; but wise
    Was Hagen, and they feared him. "I advise,"
He said, half scornful, "this strong Dragon-slayer
    To welcome friendly, lest he wrathful rise
And crush us!" So they spake the stranger fair,
Who crossed their sill and cast a splendour on the
    air.

XL.

He crossed their sill, and Gunther's soul was drawn
    In yearning to the kingly stranger's soul,
Each looked at each, and then began the dawn
    Of their strong friendship, that such joy and dole
    Should bring, for clear as on illumined scroll
Each in the other's eyes saw " brother " writ.
    The youthful kings and all the glittering shoal
Of courtiers to the guest did honour fit,
And thus for weal and woe his fate with theirs was knit.

XLI.

Now as the splendid following glanced across
    The threshold, from a narrow lattice-pane
Looked Chriemhild in the court; a blood-red floss
    Of broiding silk she chose, singing a strain
    Of careless song, but a swift sudden stain
Of crimson touched her fair cheeks' tender bloom,
    When she beheld in strange and subtle pain
Siegfried, with visor raised and floating plume,
All sheathed in burnished mail, above his warmen loom.

XLII.

She dropped her crimson floss, she stopped her song,
    She gazed with parted lip and startled eye,
    She gazed upon the dreadless hero long,
        She marked his gentle speech, his bearing high,

His kindly looks, his lofty courtesy;
And while she gazed a gently pulsing bliss
   Stole through her, till she breathed a long, long sigh,
Then turned, half fearing she had done amiss,
To Uta, whispering low, "Sweet mother, who is this?"

XLIII.

Then Siegfried many days at Worms abode,
   Welcomed as would befit a puissant king.
At times through balmy greenwood glades they rode,
   Glades flooded with the music of the spring,
   And there the fleet-foot stag to bay would bring.
At night in hall great deeds of hoary eld
   And lays of love impassioned minstrels sing;
All passing hours the friends' hearts closer weld,
But from the hero's eyes Chriemhild is ever held.

XLIV.

Days grow to weeks, weeks months, but never yet
   Hath Siegfried breathed aloud his lady's name,
Hath Siegfried longing, loyal glances set
   Upon the beauty whose far-rumoured fame
   Fired his strong soul with such enduring flame;
But from her secret bower the maiden gazed
   With stolen glance when knights for martial game
Were met in lists below; and when they praised
The stranger's skill her eyes with dewy lustre blazed.

XLV.

No longer now dim tales from far-off days
  Of fair deeds shining through the mists of time,
Her young companions' sweet and joyous lays,
  Not her well-sounded cithern's tuneful chime,
  Or garden, blooming bright in summer prime,
Much pleased her; oft at eve she mused apart,
  Or watched pale, pensive stars from hill-tops climb,
Oft at her broiding frame from dreams would start,
And blush, oft speak of things far distant from her heart.

XLVI.

Now Uta marked the change with secret joy,
  Pale Uta, mother sage and widowed queen,
Yet to her gentle child wrought no annoy
  By words, but made as if she had not seen;
  Often she spake of Siegfried, when serene,
Still hours she passed with Chriemhild and the kings;
  Then Gunther praised with the impassioned mien
Of friendship's youth his deeds and wanderings;
But Chriemhild silent heard as musing other things.

XLVII.

With seemly rivalry of noble love
  King Gunther straitly scanned his goodly friend;
He marked his grace and courtliness, and strove
  To grasp his high ideal and amend
  His own by that, and all false seeming rend

From all within and all around; yet thought
　Never to equal him, but strength to spend
In manly striving. So his soul was caught
In friendship's mighty bands, and so to high things
　　wrought.

XLVIII.

And Siegfried's heart to all the brothers clave,
　But most to Gunther. Soon the clang of arms
Rang from the east, where league-long forests wave;
　Such sound as warrior's eager spirit warms,
　Presaging peril and the glorious harms
Of foughten field. It fell upon a day
　When the young year was dressed in sweetest
　　charms,
The three Burgundian sovereigns went their way,
Heading a goodly host in war's superb array.

XLIX.

The best and bravest of their men they chose
　To try their cause in battle's desperate chance,
And Siegfried they besought to make their foes
　His own, and with his sword their cause advance,
　So, watched by maidens' stolen, shamefast glance,
As Gunther's man, by serving doubly great,
　He went. Where swift sword-lightnings fiercest
　　dance,
Waved Siegfried's plume, and oft he turned the fate
Of nicely balanced war by his sole sword-point's
　　weight.

L.

Beneath the Saxon mountains dwelt the foe,
   King Lintger ; and, to humble Burgundy,
Lintgast of Denmark he had called from snow
   And ice, beyond the ever-troubled sea ;
   So these two kings against the brothers three
Waged war. But, even to his furthest hold,
   For many days was Lintger made to flee,
And Siegfried captured Lintgast, him with gold
He chained, but set him free for goodly ransom told.

LI.

And many noble deeds of arms were done
   On both sides in this war ; the two boy-kings,
Gunther's young brothers, maiden honour won ;
   But Siegfried's glory floated on the wings
   Of rumour to the four winds' hidden springs ;
And when to Worms his deeds' renown was blown,
   So strangely sudden joy a maid's heart wrings,
Sweet Chriemhild's eyes with happy tear-drops shone,
And to her bower she fled and mused apart alone.

LII.

Twelve moons had gleamed and gloomed since Siegfried left
   His home at Santen ; now the springing year
Again blushed maid-like, and with touches deft
   The meadows broidered, made the heaven clear,

And filled the woods with music. Then drew near
The Whitsun feast, the feast of flower and song;
   At Worms the home-come victors made great cheer
With joust and revel, lasting twelve days long;
Thither from near and far flocked in a motley throng.

LIII.

How glorious broke the dawn of that fair day
   When first Prince Siegfried met his lady's eyes,
That Whitsun morn! The Niblungs' stern array
   Around the court was ranged at still sunrise;
   Before the kings the trumpets' stirring cries
Rang boldly, chamberlains in cloth of gold
   Flashed forth in glowing file, as if the skies
Had burst and all their glory earthward rolled;
Then followed high-born maids of beauty's sweetest mould.

LIV.

Last came the queen, and, leaning on her arm,
   The princess, star-like in her loveliness,
Her rich attire unmarked beside the charm
   Of her sweet beauty; bright her flowing tress
   As Niblung gold, but earthward did she press
Her looks, like one in stilly convent cell
   Who museth lone; yet, once beneath the stress

SIEGFRIED'S GLORY

Of Siegfried's glance she raised them, and the spell
Of deep undying love on those young spirits fell.

LV.

Then sudden red lit Chriemhild's gentle face,
   But Siegfried's darkened in a heavy cloud;
For when he marked the lady's lofty grace
   His heart sank low, his soul in homage bowed,
   As doubts and fears surged up in thickening crowd.
"How should I win thee, oh thou loveliest?"
   He in!y sighed, yet he was passing proud
That his long look one glance from her could wrest,
And sweetest, strongest hopes swept through his troubled breast.

LVI.

Then to the minster, over dewy grass,
   Beneath boughs fragrant with the breath of spring,
All fared, in order due, to hear the mass.
   Oh, holy place! where peasant, peer, and king,
   Maid, wife, and child bow equal; where, on wing
Of heaven-storming prayer, together rise
   So many hearts—the strong, the suffering,
Dizzy with joy or over-bowed by woes,
With souls that safe in bliss of Paradise repose!

LVII.

There Siegfried prayed for Chriemhild, she for him,
  Their souls upborne upon the surge of song,
That flooded nave and aisle and chapel dim
    With thankful praise the echoing vaults prolong
    To Him who wrought deliverance from wrong;
Loud prayed the priest; fair children, snowy-stoled,
    With looks celestial, for the kneeling throng
Swung jewelled censers chained with beamy gold,
Whence clouds of heavenly balm around the altar
    rolled.

LVIII.

And when the holy rites were fully done,
  And on the people's souls lay peace divine,
Once more the bright procession in the sun
    Ranged round the castle-yard in ordered line.
    Then Gunther, with the old time's breeding fine,
Prince Siegfried led before the royal maid
    For guerdon; lowly did the prince incline
To her, but spake no word till Chriemhild paid
Him sweet and gracious thanks for his most timely
    aid.

LIX.

Then, looking up, he saw her standing there,
  Enringed by sworded warrior, jewelled dame,
And high-born damsel, so beyond compare
    The fairest, purest, princeliest, that shame

Fell on him, and his lips to shape her name
Were fearful; but her sweet and steadfast glance
  Met his and fired in each a deathless flame.
Then said he, "Lady Chriemhild, what the chance
Of battle gave is yours; for you I lifted lance."

LX.

The lady smiled, and even as the beam
  Of earliest morn the dark sea ruby dyes,
With gradual touch on wood and shadowed stream,
  And round snow-peaks in awful splendour lies
  Till the last shadow leaves the lucid skies
And full life breathes through all the wakened earth;
  So the soft lustre of her lips and eyes
The hero touched—his pulses leapt with mirth,
His kindling features glowed with sense of life's
    new worth.

LXI.

"And must I leave thee? liever were I laid
  In loveless tomb, from sun and starshine hid."
So Siegfried to his heart in silence said.
  Then heralds to the lists the warriors bid;
  Like sunbeams in a wood, he glanced and slid
Among the heroes—all around him whirled
  Slit scarves and broken weapons. What he did
Chriemhild, with throbbing heart and lips upcurled,
In wonder saw, and tears of pride her eyelids
    pearled.

LXII.

Twelve days the revels lasted. All that time
　　The prince in Chriemhild's sight with bliss abode:
Now first he felt all things harmonious chime
　　Within him; but the hours so swiftly strode
　　The feast was done, the guests upon their road
Set forth, and sadly he to start prepared:
　　Then Gunther prayed him, by the thanks they owed,
To stay. Thus longer time their roof he shared,
But still as yet no word of winning Chriemhild dared.

Lay the Third

THE WINNING OF BRUNHILD

F

III.

PRELUDE

KNOW ye the land, not set in any sea
   Of mariner sailed with sail of mortal loom,
Where glows not fruit of any earth-grown tree,
   Where, stealing soul and sense, pale flowers bloom?

Know ye that land, so strange, so dim, so far,
   Not found on any chart by mortal limned,
Not shone upon by sun or dewy star,
   But lit with lustre night hath never dimmed?

There spread waste tracts by mortal foot untrod,
   Where fitful lightnings dart in arrowy gleams,
Where vague, weird figures brush the dewless sod,
   And voices pass unbodied as in dreams.

There jewelled palaces, by hands unwrought,
   Lift airy pinnacles from craggy heights,
Rocks cleave and lighted halls appear unsought,
   Full of sweet song and perfume and delights.

There rivers murmur low through blossomed meads,
  And whoso sips their wave is lost to pain;
Weird tales are whispered by the bending reeds,
  That whoso hears is bound in magic's chain.

There are long galleries, that wind and wind,
  Like serpents, in a dark and endless maze
Through spacious temples, where strong gods, reclined
  In joy, loom dimly through an incense haze.

And there are gardens, scented, blissful, bright,
  Dusk tangled forests, where trees speak and bleed,
Where wanders many a mailed, immortal knight
  With damsel fair from dark enchantment freed.

Set sail and grasp the tiller firm, and far,
  Through tideless, stormless seas, that marvellous land,
Unhelped by compass, chart, or pilot star,
  Seek, till the swift keel smite the waveless strand!

LAY THE THIRD

The Winning of Brunhild

I.

THERE dwelt a queen beyond the northern seas,
   A maiden queen and fair, Brunhilda hight.
Full many a goodly warrior sought to please
   That lady; but alone by mortal fight
   With her could any win the guerdon bright
Of her surpassing beauty; mortal man
   Not yet prevailed against her charmèd might;
And whom she worsted lost his head, and wan
In death lay; thus her dread through all the wide
   world ran.

II.

King Gunther heard her fame beside the Rhine,
   Of Brunhild heard at Worms, his city old;
And straight to win that lady did he pine;
   Her glorious beauty and her strength men told,
   Her gifts, her form of more than queenly mould,
But chiefly of the all-compelling charm
   Of peril, that her beauty fenced with fold
Impregnable and fraught with glorious harm,
That thrills the warrior's soul with rapture wild
   and warm.

III.

And oft in converse with the Dragon-slayer,
   His tried and trusted friend, who now abode
At Worms for love of Chriemhild, his despair
   And passioned longing for Brunhild he shewed ;
   But Siegfried bid him win her, over-rode
His doubts, and offered help in the emprise,
   For guerdon asking Chriemhild's hand bestowed;
And, this being granted, he, in travel wise,
Gave counsel how to make the quest in fitting guise.

IV.

No armoured host would he, but warriors twain,
   Hagen and Dankwart. Many nights and days
Gold-tressèd Chriemhild and her maiden train
   Consumed in shaping raiment meet to blaze
   In splendour. Silk-stuffs from the sandy ways
Of Araby, pure flax, green silk from lands
   More distant, wool and spoil of flocks that graze
Hoar ocean's opal meads and pearly sands,
She took and fashioned fair with deftly twinkling hands.

V.

Twelve suits of goodly raiment thus they made,
   For each man three. And then at last it fell
On a sweet summer morn when sunbeams played
   On blossoming vine, bright rose, and lily-bell,
   Tipped barren peak and slipped to leafy dell,

Upon the broad blue bosom of the Rhine
   The warriors sailed. To speed them with farewell
Queen Uta and the princess did incline,
Waiting with page and squire by sunny slopes of
   vine.

VI.

The warriors seaward sailed their tiny bark ;
   Siegfried the rudder held with practised hand,
Gunther the oars, and Hagen's visage dark
   Above his baldric gloomed, when, from the land
He pushed the boat; but Dankwart took his stand
Hard by the slender mast to hoist the sail;
   Long, long the ladies lingered on the strand,
Watching the vessel dwindle to a pale
Dim speck and slip within the massed air's azure
   veil.

VII.

Adown the pleasant Rhine the wanderers sailed,
   Where vine-bloom charmed the soft and delicate
   air,
Where cot and hamlet smiled, by woods half-veiled,
   Where children played, and maidens young and fair
   Sang spinning, shadowed from the summer glare;
And here on lofty crags strong towers frowned,
   And here a convent smiled at earthly care,
Striving to shut sin from its narrow bound,
Whence life's beat wave fell back with dull and
   hollow sound.

VIII.

So fared they till, with many a yawning mouth,
  Old Rhine reluctant crawled through weedy slime,
Bringing his tribute from the gentle south;
  There the green sea reared wide a crest sublime,
  Lulling the mariners with wave-rung chime;
Then Troneck Hagen turned his fiery gaze
  On Siegfried, and would know how long a time
And through what perilous and secret ways
Their bark must sail to suit the weird witch-maiden's craze.

IX.

The bright-faced hero smiled, and said: "The ways
  To me are known, brave Hagen." Then he steered
Northwest, well scanned by Hagen's burning gaze.
  Twelve days and nights the ship's course never veered,
  But on they flew, and oft the long day cheered
With song and tale of old, heroic deeds,
  Of ocean's secret lore, of creatures weird
Who draw charmed seamen to the silent meads
Below, and wreathe pale brows with dank and dripping weeds;

X.

Of still, bright palaces of burning gems
  Beneath the heaving azure's shining floor,
Of shattered masts and tempest-broken stems,
  Of treasure wrecked, deep-hid in caverns hoar,

Of silent mariners who may roam no more,
  Of fairy isles that dream on halcyon wave,
  And great fleets crushed upon a viewless shore,
Of maidens, singing wild, sweet song that lave
Their limbs in foam, they sang, while on the vessel
    drave.

XI.

But Siegfried inly mused on her who first
  Woke the deep echoes from his silent soul,
His quest, his waiting, and his year-long thirst
  For sight of her, on that first look he stole
  That Whitsun morn, when from the brilliant shoal
Of squire and dame she shone and smiled to him;
  Him seemed once more he saw the gay lists roll,
When Chriemhild thanked him and the sky waxed
    dim,
And he his service vowed to her of life and limb.

XII.

Him seemed the monsters of the deep grew mild
  When he of Chriemhild mused; her loveliness
The sea of storm, the night of dark, beguiled;
  Often he deemed the sheen of her bright tress
  Illumed the wave beneath the keel's impress,
When through the night they sped on billowed fire;
  The sparkling stars seemed jewels on her dress,
Her voice sang in the south wind's murmurous lyre,
Her breath embalmed sweet airs that fairy isles
    suspire.

XIII.

And when the twelfth sun leapt from Orient cave,
   They sailed upon a sea of rosy fire,
Beholding, doubled in the burning wave,
   A vast and glittering pile, with many a spire
   Of marble emerald green in soaring gyre,
The embattled walls linked round by towers fourscore;
   So fair a pile might Orpheus' golden lyre
In music's passion heave from magic shore,
So fair a pile man's art had never raised before.

XIV.

To Gunther, gliding from the heavy dark
   Before the dawn, these things a vision seem;
And when the rose-light deepened on the bark,
   Till rigging, spar, and sail in crimson gleam
   Were steeped, "My brother, what a wondrous dream
Is this!" he cried. To whom the prince, "These things
   Are tangible and true, not as you deem;
For this is Isenstein, fair home of kings,
That on the still wave broods, like bird with folded wings."

XV.

Then the light strengthened and the wanderers gazed
   On clear-cut pinnacle and tower tall;

But Siegfried this brave show no whit amazed,
  And, inly smiling, as they marvelled all,
  He showed the vast sweep of the outer wall,
The cunning workmanship of roof and spire,
  The bastions' strength, the spacious inmost hall,
The palaces, aglow with emerald fire,
The carven splendours wrought to still some god's
    desire.

XVI.

They gazed like dreamers bound in magic spell,
  With hands uplift towards the aërial blaze,
While deeper glories on the towers fell
  And bright sun swept away the purple haze;
  And now they traced the turrets' wildering maze
And marked the vast hall in the central fold,
  Now in the paling of the sun's new rays
The sea of crimson fire was turned to gold,
Within whose molten wave the imaged towers were
    rolled.

XVII.

From a high oriel, opening on the sea,
  Fair ladies glanced through narrow lattice pane,
And Gunther marked one, gazing loftily,
  The fairest and the tallest of the train;
  Her robe the swan's plume mocked, of silken grain
So purely white, her neck, like that of swan,
  Arched proudly, beauty-conscious, did she strain
To see the advancing bark; then waxed she wan,
Beholding it, and asked, " Whence comes that
    bright-faced man?"

XVIII.

And Gunther asked of Siegfried, " Who is she,
  That lofty lady in the snowy stole ? "
And the world-wandered prince, scanned curiously
  By Hagen, said, " Brunhild, who makes such dole
  For heroes." Then King Gunther's inmost soul
Rejoiced. And now their keel screamed up the strand,
  The windless sail flapped idly from the pole,
With Gunther's steed Prince Siegfried leapt to land,
And there as vassal stood, the stirrup in his hand.

XIX.

Now whom she asked, to Queen Brunhild replied,
  "Lady, I know him not, a hero's mould
Is his; though he as vassal stands beside
  A man of lesser thews, helm-bound with gold,
  The bright-faced man a greater chief I hold,
Such majesty is on his lucid brow,
  Such grace and dignity his form enfold;
It ill-befits that kingly head to bow
To mortal man; some prince is he, disguised by vow.

XX.

" Two warriors stand beside them, richly clad,
  Their arms are wondrous rich and all their gear,
The younger hero hath a visage glad.,
  Lightly he sits his steed and holds his spear;

Methinks the fourth was never touched by fear,
How swiftly run his glances to and fro!
  A mighty man, dark-browed, and waxing sere
  Of life; Heaven send me not his like as foe!"
So spake he, while the queen glanced, troubled-flushed, below.

XXI.

Long, long she gazed on Hagen. "As a friend
  That dark-browed man were worth a thousand more,"
She mused, then bade her men the guests attend.
  Silk stuff and gold wrought tissue, maidens bore
  From cedarn presses to the queen, with store
Of gems from stout oak coffers bound in steel;
  A kingdom's wealth upon her breast she wore,
And round her waist the girdle that should seal
The doom of Gunther's race and Siegfried's earthly weal.

XXII.

Thus, in attire that flashed like many suns
  But richlier still arrayed in beauty's light,
The strong queen came below. Around her runs
  A quick-hushed murmur, for, so bravely dight
  Is Brunhild rarely in her people's sight;
With regal mien she paced the pillared hall
  To greet the sea-borne guests; her princely height,
Her beauty's splendour and her strength appal
The wanderers, till their looks, all dazzled, downwards fall.

XXIII.

But Siegfried unabashed the war-maid's eye
  Encountered, and, advancing, her addressed;
Then she, "Who may these warriors be? and why,
  Lord Siegfried, come they?" Then the prince, her hest
Obeying, smiled, and briefly said, "'To test
His sword comes Gunther, and your hand to win;
  He is a king and I his man; the best
Of all his heroes, near to him of kin,
Is Hagen, Dankwart next. When shall the fight begin?"

XXIV.

As in a summer wood the stately trees
  Stand silently in golden glamour bound,
But, at the wakening of a little breeze,
  Their leaves lift and a whisper circles round
  From tree to tree, so went a gentle sound
Of laughter round the queen from maid to maid
  Grouped near her. Then Brunhilda, "On the ground
Where I shall fight, the bleaching bones are laid
Of many a warrior strong with shattered casque and blade.

XXV.

"Methinks the prowess of the Dragon-slayer
  Himself were hardly tried in single fight
With me! Let him betake himself to prayer
  And look his farewell on the blessèd light

Who dares assail my never-conquered might,
For that bold man must win or death or me.
Lord Siegfried, warn your master, lest the bite
Of fanged remorse your heart tear endlessly,
Well know you what to war with maiden strength may be."

XXVI.

Then angry lightning shot from Siegfried's eye,
Whereat the strong queen trembled and her hue
Waxed fainter; but the prince made calm reply
Sweet-voiced. "King Gunther knows the forfeit due
To vanquished knight; the fleshless bones that strew
The plain affright him not. Say, fairest queen,
When shall the fight begin, that we may view
As noble combat as the world hath seen?"
Then Gunther spake, whom Brunhild scanned with scornful mien.

XXVII.

So for the strife at once the swan-necked maid
Gave order, and to arm herself withdrew.
King Gunther took his spear, his limbs arrayed
In armour, girt his sword of temper true;
Siegfried the mystic robe of sightless hue
Threw on, and Balmung, his renownèd brand,
Unseen beneath his veil of darkness drew;
Then, on a space of seaward-fronting land,
Outside the emerald walls the warriors took their stand.

XXVII.

How glorious the martial maid appeared
  In helmèd splendour, when the appointed ground
Impatiently she trod. Even Hagen feared
  For Gunther, when her limbs in armour bound
  He saw, and marked the charmed hair floating round
Her supple form, and marked the cool disdain
  That shaped her firm lip's curve and mute speech found
In her far-flashing eye, the lovely bane
Of many a stalwart knight stretched stiff along the plain.

XXIX.

But deeper waxed his dread when three tall men
  A spear three-edged, long-hafted, staggering bore;
This Brunhild caught and lightly poised, as when
  Some careful housewife seeks her garnered store
  And shakes an unthreshed stalk of barley hoar;
In wrath he slipped and haste to Gunther's side
  And muttered, "Let us leave this cursed shore;
This is the Devil's wife. If we abide
We are dead men." To whom the king, "All knightly pride

XXX.

"Were put to shame if we this strife refused."
  Then Hagen grasped his sword and swore to sell
Their lives at dearest. And the young king mused
  In terror of the prize so fair and fell,

And thought how bards his timeless death would tell
In after years—a king by woman's might
   Undone. But Siegfried, hid by mystic spell,
Drew near and whispered, "All the acts of fight
Seem thou to make while I do battle out of sight."

XXXI.

Then Gunther viewed the maid with lightened cheer
   And smiled when sweating men a huge shield brought,
A mighty shield to match the mighty spear,
   Full three spans thick, of gold and iron wrought;
   The princess lightly in her white hand caught
The massy shield, and, with a pard-like bound,
   Leapt face to face with Gunther; then she sought
Her aim and launched the spear. With rushing sound
It split the air and smote a thousand sparkles round

XXXII.

From the well-balanced shield and cleft it through,
   That Siegfried staggered; but he stood again,
Then from his mighty hand the king's spear flew,
   While Gunther well-nigh swooned from the fierce strain
   Upon his hand; it smote the shield amain
That fire sprang like a fountain from the gold
   And the strong queen reeled o'er the heaving plain

G

To earth, and in the dust her tresses rolled,
Loud clanged the massive shield, shot from her palsied hold.

XXXIII.

Up leapt the warrior maid with crimsoned brow
   And flaming glance, and scornfully she spake,
"Receive my thanks, Knight Gunther, for the blow!"
   Then twelve stout men in cords that well-nigh brake
   A stone brought, which the mountain elves to make
A thousand years had sweat. This Brunhild heft
   With ease, as matrons heave a baken cake
And turn it on the coals with touches deft,
Then hurled it, that it hissed as eddying airs it cleft;

XXXIV.

And after it so many ells she sprang
   It seemed to draw her in its rapid train,
Her flowing hair flashed and her armour rang
   As she alighted far upon the plain;
   But the stone's falling all eyes sought in vain,
So far it was. Then Siegfried found the stone
   And tossed it, like a fruit that long hath lain
Grass-hid, and launched it; but it seemed alone
From Gunther's far-flung hand the massive rock was thrown.

XXXV.

Yet Siegfried heaved it; far above the queen
    And far beyond in dizzy curve it flew;
And Gunther, caught by Siegfried's arm unseen,
    With mighty spring, as if a load-stone drew
    Him after, flashed against the arching blue,
And lighted far beyond the great stone's cast.
    This Brunhild saw, and waxen wan she grew
And marvelled. Then rose voices like a blast
In sudden storm at sea when snaps the sail-bent mast.

XXXVI.

For never yet so strong and far a spring
    In sight of man by woman-born was made;
Men closed around the spot in narrowing ring,
    Applauding, mindless of the heavy shade
    Upon the fair queen's brow. Silent she stayed
Afar, most like a lovely statue raised
    By art of man, with gold and steel inlaid,
In some great city square, where joy-fires blazed,
Bells clashed, men thronged, but she on all unheeding gazed.

XXXVII.

Now Hagen marked the spring, and every hair
    Upon his flesh in bristling awe upreared.
Anon he asked himself in what fell snare
    Of devilry he with his prince had steered;
    And while he mused, the Niblung prince appeared
In his own form, unclothed of magic vest,

And sadly asked, as he some hindrance feared,
"Fair queen, when shall the fight begin?" Then pressed
The vanquished maid in shame her white hands to her breast.

XXXVIII.

"Come hither, noble knights and warriors all;
Come hither, every man of mine," she cried,
"The fight is lost and won; King Gunther call
Your lord henceforth." And all the crowd replied
With shouts. Then Gunther, flushed with joy and pride,
Drew near, and, with a mute betrothal kiss,
Encircled with his arms the glorious bride;
Then smiled the queen as nothing were amiss,
And in full-voiced acclaim thundered the people's bliss.

XXXIX.

Then the Burgundians of home-going spake,
But Brunhild: "Where are all King Gunther's men
And ships, that he may fitly homeward take
His hardly-conquered queen?" Embarrassed then
Was Gunther, but the Niblung, swift of ken
And speech, replied: "The winds and stormy waves
Delay our hosts no longer than till when
Day's king a third time in the ocean laves,
And, risen on new-yoked car, the sea with gold flake paves."

THE WINNING OF BRUNHILD

XL.

So once more in his robe of mystery veiled
  Aboard the anchored boat the Niblung leapt;
And there the people saw, and, seeing, paled,
  The ship from all her moorings suddenly swept;
  Then marked they how the sails in silence crept
About her masts, how, like a living thing,
  Unsteered, unoared, by foot of man unstept,
She lifted in the breeze her snowy wing
And fled afar, till lost in evening's purple ring.

XLI.

Now Siegfried through the night in darkness flew
  And dawn, and gained the dim and distant land
Of Niflheim; then his magic sail he drew
  Close in, and silent trod the soundless strand.
  Niblungs and dwarfs uprose at his command,
An army mustered and a gallant fleet;
  The swart dwarfs drew across the furrowed sand
Rich treasure from the hoard—gold bracelets, meet
For beauty's arm, and gems whose hearts in fire-
    dew beat,

XLII.

Rings with pure pearl and quivering diamond set,
  Rich rubies darkly bright, celestial gleam
Of sapphires, stuffs where golden broidery met
  So thick on shining silk that not the beam

Of sun in dark rooms hath so dense a stream
Of lustrous motes; these from the war-won store
   The Dragon-slayer chose; then through the cream
Of churning surf that edged the mystic shore
The vessels ploughed, and straight to Isenland they
     bore.

XXXIII.

And, when the second dawning scattered pearl
   And gold upon the blue sea's heaving floor,
They saw the night-mist break in filmy curl
   From the green-gleaming towers upon the shore;
Then Siegfried drew the coil of darkness o'er
His kingly brow and lightly leapt to land;
   First to the expectant queen tidings he bore
Of Gunther's fleet at anchor by the strand
And spoke of gifts and men, by Brunhild straitly
     scanned.

XLIV.

And when at last the richly-dowered bride
   Weighed anchor, all her fleet was girdled round
By Niblung ships, gold-laden; thus her pride
   Was amply fed. Yet many a sigh profound
   Broke from the royal maiden's bosom, bound
No more in steel but silk; and oft alone
   She sat and watched gay living things that wound
Through lucent waves, or saw the purple zone
Of heaven alight with stars like flowers on May-
     meads blown.

XLV.

Now Chriemhild, safe at home in quiet bower,
　Of those far-wandering warriors musèd oft,
And oft in secret from her kingly tower
　She gazed on glooming wood and bloom-starred croft,
　Adown the broad Rhine, till in mazes soft
Of azure air he slipped; at morn she gazed,
　While earth slept and one waning star aloft
Her lamp still swung, and when the pale moon raised
Her pearly throne at eve and hill-tops rose-red blazed.

XLVI.

Deeply she mused of perils on the seas
　By storm, by night, strange beasts and magic things
That cheat the mariner, chilly climes that freeze
　His breath, of dreadful fish with scaly wings,
　And torrid suns whose rays are serpent stings;
Often in silence she for Siegfried prayed
　And Gunther; often with the youthful kings,
Her brothers, spake she of the glorious maid,
So dreadful though so fair, and of the scanty aid

XLVII.

The king had taken. Much the brothers feared
　For Gunther; only Uta, undismayed

Of Siegfried's skill and strength spoke and his weird
   Unearthly armour, and she held his aid
   Sufficient; so the gentle princess stayed
Her hope upon this faith. Once, ere the morn,
   Out-gazing on the dim earth wrapped in shade,
She heard the lark up-spring from bending corn
In music, and afar, upon the dark wave borne,

XLVIII.

In the gray dawning saw a snowy sail
   Swift-speeding; then her heart beat; then before
The first rose reddened in the heaven pale,
   The white wings folded by the unsunned shore
   And she beheld the Dragon-slayer moor
His boat; then straight her comely limbs she laid
   Again upon her couch. The Niblung bore
Good tidings. So to greet the royal maid
They stirred and bower and hall in garlands gay arrayed.

XLIX.

The beacons flamed, the vassals dwelling round
   Sped to the sign, hot-spur, with foamy rein;
And all upon the river-fronting ground
   Stood ordered fair to greet the bridal train,
   Bending, as bends a field of ripening grain
By soft airs touched, before that glorious bride
   And groom. Then music wrought the tangled skein

Of blisses manifold to one. Great pride
Moved Gunther, floating calm on honour's fullest
    tide.

L.

And ere that sun long time had passed the
    noon,
King Gunther guerdoned for his timely aid
Prince Siegfried, eager for the promised boon,
    And in the dreadless hero's arms he laid
    The peerless-beautiful, the princely maid.
This, solemnly before the shining sun,
    In sight of all the subject lords, arrayed
In state at Worms, with noble speech was done;
There the first kiss, the kiss of troth, so strangely
    won,

LI.

Was given; nor recked they in the trembling
    bliss
    Of blended breath and meeting souls on lips
Still virgin, of a last, an anguished kiss,
    Nor of warm hearts struck down in quick eclipse
    Of death, nor of the fiercely-stinging whips
Of vengeance, nor of anything that harms;
    And, as at morn the roselight softly tips
The hill-top, then unfolds the valley's charms,
Slowly the princess flushed, close-clasped in happy
    arms.

LII.

Then from the courtly host a shout arose
   Like surges when the storm-blasts break their lair;
For never nobler, loftier hero chose
   Lady of lovelier face, or soul more fair,
   And the warm cordial love the people bare
Her grace and courtesy of years had earned;
   Even the grim Hagen wore a gentler air
When on the twain his blazing glances burned,
But Brunhild from the sight with wrathful visage turned.

LIII.

The war-maid turned, and in her lustrous eyes
   Tears rose and trembled down her fair cheek's bloom;
This Gunther marked with conscience-stung surprise,
   And bent, as shame strove in his soul's strait room
With fear, till on her drooped his helmet-plume,
Asking what sorrow touched his fairest queen.
"I weep," she cried, "thy sister's lowly doom,
That thou shouldst give her to a man so mean,
Thy vassal, and her fate of all the world be seen!"

Lay the Fourth

THE FATAL GIFTS

PRELUDE

Marriage

WHEN God man's lot on earth would chiefly bless,
  He bade him be, not one alone, but twain;
To one most power, to one most loveliness,
  Of soul and body, gave he, and with chain,

Silk-soft but strong as adamant, he bound
  Their lives. Thus yearnings in man's spirit rise
To link his strength with sweetness, and to sound
  The gentler soul that laughs from beauty's eyes

And all the rough-hewn edges of his might
  To shape in polished shafts to firmly bear
The grace of arch and turret, springing light
  Into the vast of heaven's azure air.

Nor vainly yearns he; even as sunbeams, hidden
  Long æons past in buried groves of fern,
At touch of flame, from chill and darkness bidden,
  In flame the sun's long-cherished rays return,

Love wakes at touch of love; the self-same strain
    That strength to sweetness draws for perfectness,
Draws sweetness in the coil of power's chain ;
    So lightning's opposite fires together press

For calm and safety ; fires that, held asunder,
    Deal death and ruin in their ceaseless yearning,
Each calling each with roar of rolling thunder,
    Each flashing unto each, all barriers spurning.

Love wedded is a home in life's bleak waste,
    An ingle-nook of rest from care and toil,
Where human souls in holy calm are braced,
    Refreshed, and held apart from earthly soil.

Thrice happy he in reverence due who holds
    These mysteries! upon his heaven-touched eyes,
Bright, through the clinging mist that earth enfolds,
    Visions of heavenly espousals rise.

LAY THE FOURTH

The Fatal Gifts

I.

'TWAS harvest time; upon the sunny plain
　　The corn bent heavy to the reaper's hand,
Fruits, globed in russet, gold and purple stain,
　　Through dark leaves glowed; strong arms by
　　　　August tanned
　　The cut sheaves caught and bound in straw-twist
　　　　band;
The blood rose warmer through the clustered vine;
　　Voices of mirth and labour filled the land
Day long and in the warm moon's mellow shine;
Calmly by crag and croft flowed on the emerald
　　　　Rhine.

II.

And while the tiller gathered in his store
　　From teeming earth, the war-worn Dragon-slayer
The fruit of valour reaped. The river-shore
　　At Worms was thronged by motley crowds, the air
　　By mirth and music broken; passing fair
The flower-dight city smiled, with arras quaint,
　　Pageant and masque, and armour bright and rare;

In the dim minster, rich with carven saint
And pictured angel calm, heaven's breath with sweet was faint.

III.

For now at last the bridal rites were done
    That Chriemhild to her long-tried lover gave,
And wed King Gunther to the lady won
    By occult power, the spoil of valour, brave
    As beautiful. Until the dumb, dark grave,
That swallows all, and stills in dawnless night
    Gay heart and tuneful tongue, crowned king and knave,
Should yawn for him, each warrior troth did plight
To either lady; thence was joyaunce and delight.

IV.

Nor did the thought that he had subtly won
    The charmèd maiden Siegfried's soul oppress,
Nor any slight misgiving cloud the sun
    That touched the zenith of his happiness;
    And, for he would all people in the stress
Of his deep joy might share, largesse he gave
    And scattered gold like seed, as through the press
He passed; men's voices swelled a thunder-wave,
Like roar of crashing seas that war in winding cave.

V.

How beauteous was the bridal, homeward going,
  How glowed the city in the torch-light glare;
It seemed some shining sun, all overflowing
  With glory, poured his light till he was bare
  Of beams. The princely brides, apparelled fair,
With jewelled broidery that mocked the stars,
  In beauty shone, but Chriemhild past compare;
Her joy was meek as when at last unbars
Heaven's portal high to soul sore spent in sin's wild
    wars.

VI.

Gaily before the bright and festal board
  In hall the newly-wedded warriors sate,
Each lovely bride beside her blissful lord
  Blushed flower-like—how could agony or hate
  Those radiant features mar, those eyes, elate
With softest fire? Swiftly the evening fled
  On wings of joy; with minstrel's lay of fate,
Of love and lofty deeds, with airy tread
Of dancer, festal cup, the hours too swiftly sped.

VII.

Night darkened, deepened; sounds of grief and mirth
  She hushed to peace within her balmy breast;
Beneath her fragrant wing the wearied earth
  Lay folded soft in deep and dreamy rest,

No more in lighted hall the jewelled vest
Of reveller flashed or waved the dancer's plume,
　The castle towers in dewy dark were dressed,
Sleep fed the thews of strength and beauty's bloom,
While strange, bright-vestured dreams swept through night's caverned gloom.

VIII.

Star after star his squadroned host arrayed
　Till every shining, silent watch was sped;
Fair flower-cups filled with dew, and then o'erweighed
　With bliss, each blossom bowed her dainty head;
　Gray glimmered in the east, where stars fell dead,
Day's pallid heralds; then, in primrose skies
　Rose sweet Aurora, fresh from Tithon's bed,
All blushes; in the light of her fair eyes,
Earth, ocean, air, and sky flushed red with joyed surprise.

IX.

Men woke, the sons of sorrow or of sin,
　The sceptred king, the babe a few days born;
Youths rose to labour, maids to toil and spin;
　Rich men and beggars, widows newly lorn
　And brides of yester-eve, that rose-breathed morn
From sleep's soft folding drew with tender touch,
　And they arose to rapture or to scorn;

Pale men awoke, just snatched from death's fell clutch;
Morn equal smiled on all, nor gave she one too much,

X.

Or one too little. Ere her beamy car
　Long way had climbed upon the sapphire road,
The castle gates swung wide and guests from far
　Poured in. The barbèd charger hotly trode
The lists; long galleries with beauty glowed;
Crowds gathered, all in festal raiment dight;
　Fair feasts were spread, red wine as water flowed,
Warm sunlight danced on plume and armour bright,
Touched motley, purple vair, and cloth of silver white.

XI.

Into the hall to greet the newly wed
　Flocked princes and great lords, the brother kings,
Gernot and Giselher, and she who read
　The future's secret lore, Queen Uta. Things
　Of price, arms richly wrought and jewelled rings,
They gave the brides; Chriemhild the golden hoard
　Of Niblung, won in early wanderings
From the fire-breathing dragon by his sword,
Received as morning gift from her heroic lord.

XII.

But who may paint the light of perfect gladness
　Upon that lady's pure and princely brow,
The lofty peace, untouched by shade of sadness,
　The modest tenderness, that until now
　Had slumbered? For at last she dared avow
Her glory in that peerless prince of men;
　With tears she thanked him, and she marvelled how
So great a knight was hers; and not till then
Did all life's meaning flash on Siegfried's raptured ken.

XIII.

It was a joy to see that noble pair,
　So blissful and so beautiful of mien,
Yet few could mark their outward grace, so rare
　And clear a medium to the souls serene
　And fair within, appeared their beauty's sheen;
It seemed our dark and cumbrous veil of flesh,
　Like radiant ether pure, itself unseen,
Disclosed them, unentangled by the mesh
Of frail mortality, in them so stainless fresh.

XIV.

But near them gloomed the other princely pair,
　Gunther and Brunhild. In the strong queen's eye
Blazed haughty daring, and her lofty air
　No softening showed; it seemed the marriage-tie

No meekness brought to her proud soul and high;
Most like a ruler gazed she on her lord
   And marked with scorn a cloud upon him lie,
While he her eyes like some keen-piercing sword
Avoided, yet with gifts he heaped the fair bride's
   board.

XV.

And little lightened Gunther's brow of gloom
   When he was greeted on his marriage morn;
It seemed some veil from darkly shadowed doom
   Before his eyes by fateful hand was torn;
   The down-struck glance that comes of dreaded
      scorn
Was his; and to his friend ere day waxed old,
   To Siegfried, "Woe the hour that I was born!"
He cried; "No gentle bride of human mould
Is mine, but devil's wife, let loose from Hell's black
   hold."

XVI.

He told that, when the twain were left alone,
   Brunhild her lord by strength of arm o'ercame
And helpless bound for pastime in her zone;
   This with averted face he told, and shame
   His features fired with bitter, burning flame.
But Siegfried bade him mend his cheer and he
   Would aid in cloak invisible, that blame
Of weakness should not touch him; wherefore free
From care King Gunther passed that day right
   joyously.

XVII.

But when again the pair alone were found,
  Gunther his powers in sportive fight would try;
Brunhild with scorn consented; he who bound
  The other, would through life have mastery;
Then strove the twain, and Siegfried, standing by
Unseen, the strong queen pinioned fast; then, wrought
  To fierce despair, she strove as she would die;
But Siegfried held and bound her. Thence he brought
Her girdle and her ring, of malice deeming nought.

XVIII.

Of malice deemed the dreadless warrior nought
  But mirthful aid for friendship's gentle sake;
He little recked the peril that is wrought
  By foreign aid in marriage, or the snake
  That through his well-meant friendliness should break
From deadly coil upon them. For his friend
  All lawful things would Siegfried undertake,
His dearest blood for him with gladness spend,
And all his glorious gifts with joy to aid him lend.

XIX.

—Ah, kingly Dragon-slayer, couldst thou not slay
  Thy fault of sex, male arrogance, half scorn,
Half tenderness, that makes it fair to play

With woman's rarer gifts as quips mirth-born
In Nature's wanton mood, false plumage, worn
By eagle-aping dove, that makes a lie
    To woman told a manly lip adorn,
To cheat her, kindness, purest chivalry
To male Procrustean whim her stretched, lopped
    soul to tie?—

XX.

But woe the hour when he to Chriemhild told
    The thing with smiles, and woe the fatal hour
When he the girdle gave and ring of gold
    To Chriemhild! Better were that princely flower
    Faded in bud before the deadly dower
She took, with laughing lip she took, and breast
    Untouched by guile. The Norns with viewless power
Thus wove the darksome woof when life was best;
Thus cruel death oft comes in smiles and joyance drest.

XXI.

So Gunther reaped the fruits another sowed,
    And swayed an empire by another won,
With unapt hand he swayed; and Brunhild showed
    Strange gifts, and spoke strange speech of colour dun
    And cloudy, oft his meaning would out-run,

Often her lord with mystery perplexed,
　And oft she smiled strange, joyless smiles, as one
By unstilled hungering for ever vexed;
To him some fair-limned scroll she seemed of mystic text.

XXII.

But from that night her charmèd maiden might
　Took wing, and she her weapons cast aside;
No more the plumed helm throned above her bright
　And thoughtful eyes; no more in martial pride
　She hurled the spear or cast the swift stone wide,
No more her tender breast in iron bound;
　With busy hand the distaff now she plied,
About her radiant brow fair flowers she wound,
And in all woman's arts and skills was perfect found.

XXIII.

Now sped the bridals merrily, and first
　Was Siegfried, as of yore, in martial game.
With Gunther oft he strove, and always worst
　Was Gunther, but in failing felt no shame;
　Nor did prince Siegfried prize the bloodless fame
Of tilting ground; but much he loved to see
　His prowess set his lady's cheek aflame,
And once he marked Brunhild, and saw that she
Behind her wimple's fold was weeping silently.

XXIV.

Why wept the fair queen? Who the complex strands
   Of woman's thought to certain source may trace?
What clue contrived by lightest, deftest hands
   May find that labyrinthine hiding place?
   The bright tears dimmed the beauty of her face,
Her soul the splendid jousts a burden found;
   Unto her lord she said, "The evil case
Of Chriemhild grieves me, to a vassal bound;
Alas! in what sad coil hast thou thy sister wound!"

XXV.

Then Gunther, flushing, "Siegfried is a king,
   And glorious hero tried in hard emprise,
In after-time high bards his fame will sing,
   Undying light about his name will rise."
   And Brunhild, "Mystery around us lies;
Not as a king this man thy stirrup held;
   Thou, lord of all this realm, in nobler wise
Shouldst mate thy sister; better were she celled
In convent gloom than thus to lowly fate compelled!"

XXVI.

And ever when they spoke of Siegfried's fame
   Or Chriemhild's beauty, waxed the fair queen's grief,
And when she marked their eyes in holy flame
   Of love together burn, like autumn's leaf

Her rose-lip quivered, and her soul reprief
In scornful looks found; yet she spake them fair,
And Chriemhild sister called, and mourned their brief
Sojourn in Worms. But when beyond compare
Chriemhild her hero praised, how changed the Valkyr's air!

XXVII.

But Chriemhild nothing recked of wrath or pain
So pure a light of love about her lay;
Each fleeting moment brought her deeper gain
Of joy, and Siegfried every dawning day
Made closer and of greater price; thus gay
As never in life's rosy dawn was she;
And, if her early dreams their pinions gray
Flapped through the chambers of her memory,
She mused with hope and joy Queen Uta's prophecy.

XXVIII.

Queen Uta's prophecy, that such a cup
Of bliss, as never woman sipped before,
For her through warrior's love should sparkle up
To foaming brim and even overpour
In benediction. Then the wan queen's lore
With smiles she praised; and Uta, what of woe
The dream foretold, to show her child forbore;

Only she said at parting, "Should some blow
Of evil hap thee smite— so brief is bliss below—

XXIX.

"Think on thy mother and thy childhood's home
   And fly, hurt fledgling, to thine early nest."
But Chriemhild smiled ; she deemed the transient foam,
   That crowns the cup from life's first vintage pressed
   Immortal ; thus, in perfect gladness dressed
As in an armour, sorrow she defied ;
   And thus the festal hours with perfect zest
Enjoyed, and at her worshipped lover's side
Moved softly down the stream of joy's full-flowing tide.

XXX.

Oh! happy days, youth's golden, glorious prime,
   Oh ! dulcet chord of mutual love, that binds
Discording elements to purest chime
   Of music ! Happy he who early finds
   That bliss, while glamour still young vision blinds,
Thrice happy he ! though sorrow's heavy pall
   Him shadow, though chill blasts of blighting winds
On all his blossomed hopes in fury fall,
In memory still pure joys come trooping at his call.

XXXI.

Joy is a blossom from immortal bowers,
    It cannot die, though oft it seem to fade,
Though oft the glory of its Eden flowers,
    Pass from us, ere they long enough have stayed
    To glass their beauty in the eyes' still shade;
Once tasted, bliss is ours for evermore;
    In lonely nights, when earth to sleep is laid,
And pain hath clutched the sleeper's temples hoar,
Past joys with amaranth crowned steal through thought's fast-sealed door.

XXXII.

And oft the pilgrim on life's desert way,
    Forspent with travel, pauses for a space,
All smitten by the noon-tide's piercing ray,
    The while his sun-dazed eyes a resting place
    Seek in the fairy fields of youthful grace,
That lie so far behind; and there he views
    Departed joy's young smiling angel-face;
He gazes long, he will not lightly lose
That vision sweet arrayed in morn's aërial hues.

XXXIII.

At last the bride-feast ended; Sigelind's son
    His new-wed wife in state to Santen bore;

To Santen, where the Rhine-waves slower run;
  Where in great honour dwelt King Sigmund, hoar
With years and full-ripe wisdom. Not before
Had Sigmund seen so fair a bride and sweet;
  And now was ended all their longing sore,
All care and fear for Siegfried's weal; complete
Were now all earthly hopes; and now to make him meet

XXXIV.

For loftier life beyond the senses' bound
  Was Sigmund's only care; he cast away
His sceptre and his weary brow discrowned;
  Into his son's strong hand his kingdom's sway
  He gave, and near him in an abbey gray
Abode with Sigelind. Thus a double realm
  Chriemhild with Siegfried shared, and day by day
Enwreathed him as the wifely vine her elm;
And with a firm bold hand he grasped his two-fold helm.

XXXV.

In honour, peace, and bliss long time abode
  That gentle pair, with life's best treasure blest.
Mild was their sway and just; all things men sowed
  They reaped, nor dared the strong the weak molest,

King Siegfried every wrong with might redressed,
And the far land of mystic Niflheim well
He ruled. And, ere a second time they pressed
The ripened vintage or the red leaf fell,
Chriemhild a son bore, fair as pink-lipped ocean
    shell.

Lay the Fifth

THE STRIFE OF THE SISTER QUEENS

V.

PRELUDE

The Best Land*

TELL me the sweetest, fairest spot of earth,
    Tell me the land of every land most blest;
Lies it beyond the morning's rosy birth?
    Lies it beyond the crimson-pillared west?

Smiles it upon the broad earth's burning zone,
    Where chilling blasts of north wind never come?
Is it some fairy isle whose sweets are blown
    Far over sea by zephyrs soft and dumb?

Is it some still, enchantèd vale of rest,
    Deep in the heart of Alpine mountains old,
Where sunny peaks their image in the breast,
    Liquid and still, of sapphire lakes behold?

Is it some land of endless afternoon,
    Where dreamers eat the mystic Lotos-flower?
Is it the spot, beheld in magic swoon
    Or visioned trance, of Adam's primal bower?

No; 'tis the land, the land that gave us birth,
    No; 'tis the blessèd land where first we breathed,
Where first we wept, where first unconscious mirth
    Smiles with the baby's tender dimples wreathed.

'Tis the sweet land our growing limbs that fed,
　The land that gave us thews and hearts of men,
Where beauty first upon our soul was shed,
　Where Heaven opened first upon our ken.

That land whose features formed our spirits' mould,
　Whose soul to ours with earliest breath we drew,
Where first we saw the seasons' pomp unfold,
　Saw morning's splendour, evening stars and dew.

Where human care our young souls fenced from pain,
　Where human love closed round us like a tower,
Whose skies above us bent in sun or rain,
　On whose green sod we plucked life's earliest flower.

That land whose speech our earliest faltering prayer
　Bore up to Heaven and clothed our infant thought,
Shaped the dim songs of childhood's twilight air,
　Love's earliest thrills to fit expression wrought.

That is the fairest, sweetest spot of earth,
　Fertile and fresh, or parched with burning drouth,
Rich vale of beauty, craggy land of dearth,
　Bare northern peak, or rich and lustrous south.

That land the exile's heart with yearning fills,
　Hearing its tongue beneath unhomely skies,
Where Nature's glory, throned on mighty hills,
　Fair smiling plains, or seas, around him lies.

THE BEST LAND

England! a stronger yearning to thy shore
   Thy brave, world-wandering sons for ever calls
Than any land's ; the great sun's golden ore
   Unceasing on thy scattered children falls;

Yet is their England never aught than home,
   Though in far lands bloom children, brothers sleep,
To that far island-speck upon the foam
   From fairest climes they turn with longings deep.

Sweet to the pilgrim, fresh from burning Ind,
   Rise thy pale cliffs above the azure sea ;
Sweet over thymy downs the moist, west wind
   Comes wafted, sweetly smiles the shadowed lea ;

Sweet is the hoary steeple to his eyes ;
   The straggling village, deep in garden bloom ;
Wild tangled hedge-bank, whence tall elms arise ;
   Noon's chastened sunbeams, twilight's dewy gloom.

What memories on his eager spirit throng,
   What dim, strange thoughts from childhood's far abyss !
He sees what he has seen in dreams so long,
   He fears to wake lest he his joy should miss.

So deems the child of England, deeply blest
   To press once more her velvet, verdant sod,
To lay his head upon her mighty breast,
   What time his spirit wings its way to God.

LAY THE FIFTH

The Strife of the Sister Queens

I.

BRUNHILD, the bride of valour, won by might
    Not mortal, dwelt at Worms beside her king,
Ten peaceful years; a man-child, Siegfried hight,
    She bore King Gunther. Time's unresting wing
    Her beauty dimmed not, nor the ancient sting
Of life's young anguish dulled; at evening oft
    Or morn, in converse with her lord, one string
Of memory she waked with touches soft;
This theme he shunned, as hawk, in circle poised aloft,

II.

Unwelcome quarry shuns, and, to the fist
    Of patient trainer lured and loosed once more,
Again avoids; yet Brunhild never missed
    Her purpose; of the pleasant days of yore
    She spoke; how Gunther first the towered shore
Of Isenland beheld, the glorious fight
    That won her, and the noble fleet that bore
The spoil of arms to Worms; the ring, the night
That lost it; all the charm of memoried delight.

III.

"That thou thy sister to thy vassal wed,
   To Siegfried, ever grieved me," she would say,
"Yet much I marvel at their pride; his head
   In homage he not bows, nor doth he pay
   Us tribute; summers ten have passed away
Yet thou thy lawful due requirest not."
   Then Gunther, "In far lands he holdeth sway,
'T were marvel did he seek this distant spot,
Great cares and kingly toils are fallen to Siegfried's
   lot."

IV.

But in the end the woman's will prevailed;
   Gunther took counsel of his brothers twain,
Gernot and Giselher, but subtly veiled
   The purpose of the queen. To clasp again
   Chriemhild and link afresh the holy chain
Of blood and friendship that so straitly bound
   Them to the Dragon-slayer, Brunhild would fain
Behold them; then fit messengers were found;
Thus in the iris woof Norns threads of blackness
   wound.

V.

Now, after journeying many a weary day,
   The messengers the dim and distant strand
Of Niflheim reached; and welcome as the May
   In wintry climes, were men from Chriemhild's
     land

To Siegfried; and they did their lord's command;
Said he would see his brother's face once more
　At the high feast the olden usage planned,
What time the sun turned on the height and bore
Back southward, filling barn and press with bounteous store.

VI.

Then Siegfried's heart with honest gladness leapt,
　Not deeming aught of Brunhild's hidden scorn,
Or Brunhild's hidden wrath, that never slept;
　He joyed that Gunther all those years had worn
　So true a friendship, and, upon the morn
When first his eyes the pure and princely grace
　Of Chriemhild saw, he mused, and pleasure born
Of freshened memory held him for a space;
Then to the queen he told the thing with eager face.

VII.

Then rosy dyes the queen's fair cheek suffuse
　At thought of seeing home and kin once more;
Her gentle eyes brimmed up with blissful dews
　At Brunhild's kindness; memories of yore,
　Like odour of dried roses, floated o'er
Her soul, and she her lord with urgence prayed
　To bear her to the Rhine's remembered shore;
Of peril and long absence, undismayed
She heard, so they with joy all plans for travel made.

VIII.

First to Dwarf Alberich Siegfried gave the helm
    Of Niblung's mystic land, with all its gold,
To keep for him ; then, his paternal realm
    Of Santen, to a man of wisdom old
    But youthful strength, he gave in trust to hold ;
Then many wains with noble gifts were piled,
    Arms, gems, and precious stuffs of heavy fold.
Thus fared they forth, and Chriemhild's nine year's child,
Gunther, beside her rode and on the warriors smiled.

IX.

And near them came the agèd father king,
    Sigmund, with Sigelind, in a litter borne.
The ever-circling year had passed the spring,
    Warm winds swept verdant seas of billowing corn,
    The rose's heart of splendour hid the thorn,
In darkling woods the nightingale was mute ;
    But still the throstle charmed the awaking morn,
And still at eve was heard the blackbird's flute,
Warmly on woodland banks lurked gold and crimson fruit :

X.

And all day long the lark's sweet, soaring choir
    Through heaven's deeps were borne on waves of song ;
Anon a voice in rapture would expire

And drop the minstrel; so, shot from a throng
Of frosty stars, some bright orb sweeps along
The blue and falls; the honey-scented breeze
   Green meadows skimmed, where mowers, brown
      and strong,
Long, blooming swathes swept down with measured
      ease;
The woodbine's delicate horn poured sweets beneath
      green trees;

XI.

Night's balmy veil scarce dusked the dreaming
      world,
   The dead day smiled till dawn in heavens pale,
The short, smooth sward with scanty dew was
      pearled,
   Scarce had the north star seen the secret dale
   Ere the young morning made a silvery trail
Along the east; at bright and breathless noon
   A planted spear no shadow made, a sail
One thin line cast beneath it; all aswoon
With rapture, life seemed, lulled by hidden brook's
      low croon.

XII.

By land and sea, by day and night, they fared
   All in the summer's blue and balmy prime;
Strange towns they saw, from towers strange
      faces glared,
   Anon they marked white summits heavenward
      climb,

Anon on sunny slopes balm-breathing thyme
Their steeds trod; then some shadowy woodland
    dell
They entered, grateful; now the gentle chime
They heard afar of consecrated bell,
And now from hill-top caught far ocean's azure
    swell.

XIII.

So in the glowing heart of glorious June,
    Home-lands they reached and unforgotten meads,
Where spinners sang at cottage doors the tune
    That Chriemhild hushed her child with; even
        the weeds
    These wore, recalled old times and kindly deeds
In childhood; then she told her eager son,
    "This road straight onward through the city
        leads,
And yonder Rhine's fair shining waters run,
And yonder rise the towers where me thy father
    won."

XIV.

But ere they reached the city's bastioned gate,
    They marked afar a host in splendour gleam
Around the brother kings; these seeing them,
    straight
    King Gunther spurred ahead. And now a
        dream

To Chriemhild all the vanished ten years seem ;
Once more she sees her kinsmen face to face,
  Once more her father's towers, the child-loved stream
Of Rhine ; and all the sweet remembered grace
Of maiden days came back and held her for a space.

XV.

Then the kings, 'lighted to the flower-strewn ground,
  The friend of blissful youth with joy received,
And Siegfried's gold-haired son King Gunther wound
  In loving arms and high in air upheaved ;
  All spoke, but none replied, and sighs relieved
The over-joy. And each in his degree,
  The kingly parents, and the guards gold-greaved
From Niflheim, the kings welcomed cordially ;
Then through the city passed the goodly company.

XVI.

The city, all abloom with fresh-cut flowers,
  And flower-like faces, crowning gallery
And casement ; there blank walls and glooming towers
  Shone rich with golden-folded tapestry.
  Liege citizens of high and low degree
The humming streets with cheerful faces lined,
  And goodly knights and ladies fair to see,

Their heads in gracious reverence inclined
From carven balconies with silks and garlands
    twined.

XVII.

Like to the light of myriad gleaming stars
    In winter midnight, shone the liquid eyes
Of all those ladies; like faint-rumoured wars
    From distant lands, like hidden seas, that rise
    And fall unseen in full-toned symphonies
Beneath tall cliffs, arose the deep strong hum
    Of men's hushed voices; now it broke to cries
And fell; and now the strangers nearer come,
And now the Niblung's child with awed delight is
    dumb.

XVIII.

Here maidens showered blossoms, children wept
    To see the hero, who the dragon slew,
And the strange glittering guards, who proudly
    swept
    Along with all the treasure. Chriemhild threw
    Rich largesse, smiling; many a face she knew;
Brides newly pledged, who erst as children
    played
    At her betrothal; long-limbed lads, who drew
Their earliest breath; a matron, then a maid
Betrothed, whom now a band of lusty sons
    obeyed.

XIX.

At last they paused before the hoary towers
    Of Chriemhild's early home beside the Rhine,
There with her dames, a rose among bright flowers,
    Stood Brunhild ; sworded men in ordered line
    A quivering steelflash made, and many a mine
Had yawned to deck the throng with lustre rare ;
    Siegfried, Brunhilda's child of summers nine,
Smiled there with roguish eyes and sunny hair
By Uta ; blunted arms the little warrior bare.

XX.

Down from her palfrey Chriemhild lighted swift,
    Long in her arms the widowed queen she pressed
With happy tears ; anon she stooped to lift
    Brunhild's young warrior to her heart and blessed
    The lad, while Uta Siegfried's son caressed ;
Thus made they very joyous cheer, and bliss
    Grew on them ; thus no boding stirred the breast
Of Chriemhild, meeting Brunhild's gentle kiss,
Nor felt she on her lips the traitor's burning hiss.

XXI.

But Uta marked with awe the lifting veil
    Of future things ; upon her queenly child,
On Chriemhild, wistfully she gazed, and, pale
    With present joy and coming woe, she smiled.

Gunther, with restless foot and glances wild,
Paced swiftly, like a boy in forest hoar
　At eve entangled and by tales beguiled
Of dim enchantment ; thus sweet things of yore
That Siegfried brought to mind in secret dread he bore.

XXII.

But this the Niblung marked not, full of joy
　As when he won his loved and lovely dream ;
Life's fairy gold, unmingled with alloy,
　Before him flashed its soft, alluring beam ;
　Deeply he drank the fair, full-flowing stream
Of youth's far-dreamed and manhood's actual bliss,
　And with his friend he touched the gracious theme
Of young enthusiasms, plans of his
For good of man, fulfilled ; but Gunther heard amiss.

XXIII.

For all his thought was set on Brunhild's words,
　Lest she some spark of unextinguished hate
Might fire, and from her lips him seemed that swords
　Leapt piercing, and this fear a mountain weight
　Pressed on him. Oft he saw, when night grew late
And sleep weighed heavy on his out-watched eyes,
　Dread visions stalk along with tragic gait,
And, dreaming, clutched his sword, dreaming, with cries
Awoke to see the morn from rosy mist-folds rise.

XXIV.

But, as the days passed peaceful, quiet grew
    Upon him, and these things, like deeds of old
By minstrel sung, waxed faint and dim of hue,
    And Gunther's spirit took its ancient hold
Of life.   Afar on crest of hill, or wold,
High-lying, flamed the mystic summer fires,
    The night the sun his chariot turned and rolled
Slant southward; cressets lit the city spires;
Men feasted, as of old, their god-descended sires

XXV.

Had feasted, ere the gentle Christian lore
    Tamed all the world; but softer were the rites
They practised now than in the pagan yore;
    The city ways were full of wondrous sights,
    Of cunning pageantries and quaint delights;
Before the kings high jousts of arms were held,
    Fair dames of noble blood contending knights
With smiles and spirit-kindling looks beheld;
· Such gorgeous revelry oft pleased the dim, rich eld.

XXVI.

But, amid all the feasting, darkly grew
    The web of fear.   Though Brunhild's wrath and
        scorn
A loving semblance wore to outward view,
    Deep in her breast she hid the fretting thorn,

And oft to Chriemhild spoke she of the morn
When Gunther brought her to the Rhineland
  shore,
And all the pleasant time when first was born
Their friendship, of the marriage feast, the store
Of bliss that heaped their lot with blessings
  brimming o'er.

XXVII.

It chanced one day in hall the fair queens span,
  Watching hard by their sturdy lads at play ;
When, roused from thought, said Chriemhild—
  " Such a man
  Is mine, methinks by right the kingly sway
  Of many lands were his, him might obey
Great kings with honour ; how so great a one
  Is mine, I know not." Then Brunhild no way
To breathe her anger found ; what she had spun
She spoiled; from tight-clenched hands she made
  the red blood run.

XXVIII.

This Chriemhild marked not in her deep content,
  But, glancing through the open lattice-bars,
She saw the kings as they a-hawking went
  And said, "A brilliant moon among pale stars
  Siegfried with other heroes rides ; great wars
And valorous deeds have never marred the grace
  Of youth upon him." Then the ancient scars

Of hate burst open; all her beauteous face
By fury changed, her deep breaths battling with
    the lace

XXIX.

That bound her bosom, Brunhild fiercely cried,
  "Wide lands are Gunther's. He is greater far
Than Siegfried—much I marvel at thy pride,
    Thou vassal's wife! When Gunther came to war
    For me, Siegfried his vassal stood. A star,
A little falling star beneath the moon,
  Is he by Gunther!"—"Let us leave to mar
Our love by words soon said but not so soon
Forgot," Chriemhild replied, wan-hued as in a
    swoon;

XXX.

"Yet to no vassal me my brothers wed,
  Of other things, dear sister, let us tell."
Thus Siegfried's gentle wife would fain have led
    The angered queen to sweeter thoughts and well
    Have ended; but the fierce, tempestuous swell
Of passion in the Valkyr not so soon
  Might she subdue; as light, in hollow cell
Pent up, the surging ocean from the moon
With human hands restrain, or hold at highest noon

XXXI.

The sun's bright chargers from their downward path
  To evening's glowing gates, as seek to hold
In check the torrent of Brunhilda's wrath,
    That from her lips in burning passion rolled;

"I will not speak of aught till I have told
Thy husband's state; he is, and aye shall be,
  Our vassal. Tribute he shall pay of gold
And service; such King Gunther, save for thee,
Long since had claimed by arms; our vassal still
    is he."

XXXII.

This Chriemhild heard with breathless, mute
    amaze
And marvelled, was she of her wits bereaved,
That haughty queen? and in her azure eyes
  Some righteous anger shone, and sorrow heaved
  Her bosom as she said, "Thou art deceived,
Dear sister; Siegfried is the mightiest man
  And noblest hero ever breath received;
A stripling, ere his manhood's spring began,
Such deeds he wrought as not in life's full summer
    can

XXXIII.

"My brother. What he wrought will babes unborn
  In after-ages sing; the realms he won
Are greater far than Gunther's; treasures torn
  From awful powers are his; no mother's son
  Can match with him in aught that he has done.
Oft have I marvelled Gunther yields him naught
  In tribute; yet wouldst thou this topic shun

Didst thou once know what Siegfried's arm hath
    wrought
For Gunther in old times—in this thou art
    untaught."

XXXIV.

Then waxed the strong queen's wrath; her
    spinning, rent
  In fury, she cast down; her nostril fine,
Dilating, quivered; all her breath was spent
  In thickly-coming gasps; the lovely line
  That traced her bosom's curve moved like the
    Rhine,
Storm-smitten; thus, beneath an arch's spring,
  She stood erect with darkly flashing eyne,
One white arm spread abroad, like opened wing
For flight, and barbed her words with anger's
    fiercest sting.

XXXV.

"Thou vassal's wife! will nothing bate thy pride?
  Deceived? The word is thine. Before the face
Of all the people let our cause be tried;
  Then shalt thou see which takes the foremost
    place,
  Then shalt thou see and hide thy soul's disgrace
In grief. The vassal's wife shall not precede
  The reigning queen. Oft have I grieved how base
Thy lot is, lowly wed. Of royal seed
Thou comest, but thy fall with meekness thou
    shouldst heed."

XXXVI.

Then Chriemhild's lovely lip the unlovely curve
   Of wrath took, when she heard the furious queen;
Deep in her breast she felt the giddy swerve
   Of passion, burning words of bitter spleen
   Arose; but this she calmed, and spoke serene;
"So be it! When the people throng to mass
   To-morrow at the minster, let the scene
Be played. We twain upon the plot of grass
Will meet, and she is first who first the gates shall pass."

XXXVII.

Thus the first striving of the sister queens
   Arose and burst in fury not to die.
Meanwhile the princely boys at play, to scenes
   Of women's wrath unused, stood troubled by
   And let the mimic targe and helmet lie;
The maidens stood with pallid lips, and fear
   Their breath caught, when along the vaulting high
The angered queen's voice rang in echoes clear,
Of meaning dimly guessed, yet boding evil near.

XXXVIII.

Then Brunhild from the hall in anger swept,
   Her eyes scorn-flashing, and her ladies rose
And followed; but Chriemhild her station kept,
   Deep musing.—In the pane the still sun glows

Through liquid ruby stains, blood drops it throws
Upon the folded lilies of her hands,—
Until at last she turned and changed her pose,
Like one who breaks from some dread vision's bands,
Or marks a foe close couched in far and friendless lands.

XXXIX.

She stood beside a pillar, marble-still,
　The native glories of her gold hair crowned
Her gentle beauty, and her young son, ill
　Dim-boding, with his arms her tall form wound;
　A red stain lay upon the rush-strewn ground,
Upon her robe's gold fringe, upon the chair,
　Rich-carven. Her the mother queen thus found,
Queen Uta; ere the thing was past repair,
She sought to heal the strife with gentle words and fair.

XL.

Then Chriemhild, hearkening, stroked the sunny hair
　Of her young son;—so stood she there of old,
When her great beauty was but promise fair,
　So stood she there and doubtful visions told,
　Unwitting all the glory that should fold
Her future days; and Uta, heavenly-wise,
　The truth saw, and the mystic dream unrolled
Before the maiden's charmed and startled eyes,
Then coming joys she saw in sweet and still surprise;

XLI.

Yet the vague words that Uta breathed of woe,
  Far-darkening, in her joy she heeded not;
So faint the images of sorrow show
  To eyes youth-dewy, so the central spot
  Of Hope by youthful bows is straightly shot;—
These, warning, Uta breathed again, that fear
  Might hold Chriemhild, by wrath her blissful lot
To mar not. But her gentle soul was clear
And still, as after noon's wild storm, a star-strewn
    mere.

XLII.

For what of evil in the lady dwelt
  Lay hidden in the innermost recess
Of her sweet soul, dark, silent, still unfelt;
  Nor did Chriemhild that germ's existence guess,
  Or dream that some far day in bitterness
It might awake; not lightly did she brook
  Hard thought of others; rather to caress
Than curse her lips their lovely curving took;
Thus, pitying, Brunhild's wrath from memory she
    shook.

XLIII.

So from her spotless plume a snowy swan,
  Unruffled, water-drops in gliding throws;
She deemed some thoughtless word of hers began
  Her sister's wrath; thus, when at morn she rose

With soul renewed by still and soft repose,
Her orisons she said at dewy prime,
　Unvexed by shade of wrath ; so flowers unclose
In sunlight, so the lark his matin chime
Rings out in joy unreached by poet's sweetest rhyme.

XLIV.

Then wended she with all her gracious train
　Of high-born ladies solemnly to mass ;
Fair thoughts were hers and holy, not one vain
　Or evil thing the portal pure might pass
　Of her well-guarded soul ; as in a glass
Unshadowed she her inmost sins reviewed ;
　Thus, full of thought, she reached the plot of grass
Before the minster, still by night bedewed,
And passed the waiting throngs with modest grace endued.

XLV.

The folk stood back to yield the gentle queen
　Free passage ; then she raised her eyes awhile
And saw all fresh in morning's golden sheen
　The lofty glories of the noble pile ;
　Thence mighty angels bent, with tender smile
And yearning wings outspread ; there martyrs calm
　In high-poised niche rejoiced ; there from an isle
Of jewelled gold the Mother-Maid breathed balm,
There sweet-faced saints adored God's child with folded palm.

XLVI.

There prayer breathed through massive walls of
    stone,
From fretted pinnacle that pierced the sky,
From light-winged buttress, blossom-beaded zone
    Round clustered shafts, from tower embattled high;
    Carved birds and squirrels, hidden daintily
In leaf-entangled fruit, still prayer breathed;
    There marbles pure of richly various dye,
Deep-yawning arches, pillars flower-wreathed,
Praised God in beauty—yet beneath men's passions
    seethed.

XLVII.

And there before the solemn majesty
    Of that far-soaring pile of sculptured stone,
In hearing of the deep-voiced harmony
    That flooded all the aisles with heaven-sweet tone,
    Now loud, now soft, like roar of billows blown
Far over storm-swept downs, stood Brunhild, rich
    Of raiment, wrathful pale; her dark eyes shone,
Stern-purposed; she was strung to resolute pitch,
Nor marked she saintly looks above in carven niche.

XLVIII.

But marked was she of all the hurrying crowd,
    As each one, passing, rev'rence loyal made
Till Chriemhild came. Then cried Brunhild aloud,
    Advancing, that the train perforce was stayed

And the crowd stopped, as one to stop them bade,
To Chriemhild's face, Brunhild cried, "Stop! before
The queen a vassal may not go!" Affrayed,
The ladies in each following trembled sore,
While Brunhild turned, and passed towards the
    deep-arched door.

XLIX.

Now Chriemhild paused, from holy musing torn
  So roughly; Chriemhild paused, erect and pale;
Tumultuous throbs her heart shook, wrath, pride-
    born,
  Her deep eyes lit beneath her backward veil,
  Wind-tossed; quick breaths that boded coming
    bale
Escaped her nostril fine and close-pressed lips;
  Transformed was she, as, in enchanter's tale
Some lovely lady, when her beauty slips
Away at soft-waved wand, by passion's dread
    eclipse.

L.

Oh, gentle lady, better never born
  Wert thou than meeting thus thy crucial hour!
Where was thine angel guard, that summer morn,
  That he not quenched this wrath with instant
    power,
  Nor snatched thee hence to dizzy-heighted tower
Before thy lips the fatal secret spoke?
  Far better wert thou faded ere thy flower,

Before this sudden anger from thee broke,
The spark that hissing flame from smouldering
  embers woke.

LI.

Was it Chriemhild that spake, Chriemhild, indeed,
  The gentle queen, unapt to wrath and scorn?
Why swayed her body like wind-smitten reed,
  When sudden tempest o'er the lake is borne?
What visioned beauty from her face was torn,
What wild, fierce spirit in her sweet eyes burned?
  Ay me! had she from speech that fateful morn
Her anger held! Far lighter backward turned
Blown flames in ripened corn than woman's wrath
  well-earned.

LII.

Her passion burst as music from a lyre,
  Impassive, rudely struck by skilless hand,
In keen, cold speech that kindled deathless fire
  In Brunhild's soul, as flint and steel a brand
  With sharp swift strokes enflame until some land
Is wasted. "Better hadst thou held thy peace,"
  She cried, and Brunhild, startled, turned to stand
Before her, and the crowd with swift increase
Of wonder saw the dawn of hate that could not
  cease.

LIII.

"Far better hadst thou held thy peace to-day!"
  She cried, her breath with gusts of passion torn,
"For, is Siegfried a vassal, yet obey
  Him must thou as thy master. He with scorn

Thy love unvalued and unasked hath borne ;
Then twice he overcame thee, thee he bound
   For Gunther, when upon his marriage-morn
The humbled king in shame and grief he found—
I would thou hadst not stung my soul the thing
     to sound

LIV.

" Before the world ! I would thou hadst not stirred
   This passion in me ! Oh ! my friend, believe
Without my will escaped this bitter word,
   The word thy madness asked. I grieve, I grieve,
   That I have let the fatal secret leave
My guarded lips. Oh ! let us once again
   Be kind, and do not thou, I pray, bereave
My heart of love ; but let us wash the stain
Of wrath with tears away from friendship's hallowed
     chain."

LV.

Thus the fair queen, repenting ere the close
   Of that strong passion's burst ; regretful tears
Dew-sparkles made upon the velvet rose
   Of her pure cheek, and all her soul with fears
   Was tossed. But Brunhild, like some sage who
     hears
In trance the doom of nations, marble pale
   And rigid stood ; it seemed a thousand spears
Her bosom smote ; then suddenly the veil
That dimmed past things her eyes left. Like a
     gale

LVI.

Her fury smote her—scorned, deceived, undone,
  As woman, queen, and warrior betrayed,
And now, in sight of morning's clear-eyed sun,
  Her agony before her people laid!
Her heart's best blood she willingly had paid
To win one hour of charmèd strength again,
  One hour to be the glorious warrior maid,
Who made great heroes bite the bloody plain
And mowed thick ranks of war like autumn's red-ripe grain.

LVII.

So struck to stone she stood; the turning scale
  Of Chriemhild's poured-out wrath she heeded not,
Like infant touches spent on coats of mail
  The gentle queen's soft words upon her hot
  And heavy senses fell. Then crimson shot
Athwart her dusk-pale cheek, as pitying eyes
  Met hers, and suddenly the hateful spot
She left, she knew not how; but stifled cries
Torn from her deep soul rose through holy symphonies.

LVIII.

Thus the blest mysteries with unblest soul
  The sister-queens beheld; with tears and sighs
Chriemhild; but Brunhild's deep and deadly dole
  Escaped not through her passion-blazing eyes;

She heard the sweet, strong-chanted prayers rise
And float among the ribs of vaulted stone ;
She heard impatient, while fierce agonies
Her breast gnawed, while men's furtive glances thrown
Towards her, made her soul, deep-wounded, inly moan.

LIX.

A century it seemed those pains of hell
  Tore Brunhild, while she heard the chanted prayer;
Then suddenly a doubt upon her fell
  That Chriemhild's words were but the stormy air
  Of woman's wrath, and thus she left despair ;
And when the mass was ended, at the door
  She stood to face her foe, and bade her swear
Her words the bitter fruit of wrath that bore
Her over bounds of truth, harsh railing, nothing more.

LX.

Then Chriemhild, gnawed by grief and gentle ruth
  For the wan queen, a moment paused in doubt,
And mused if she upon that deadly truth
  A veil should throw, and, while thus tossed about
  With thoughts, she spoke not. Then the bitter flout
Of Brunhild came again, "Speak, vassal's wife,"
  She cried, "and pass, and let my people out,

Who wait behind thee." Like a keen-edged knife,
Straight plunged in beating breast, the words stabbed; thus the strife,

LXI.

A moment stilled, burned fiercer. Then again
   Chriemhild the secret spoke, and Brunhild cried
For proof; and now so sorely burned the pain
   Within her, well-nigh swooned she at the side
   Of Chriemhild, ere the angered queen replied,
" Thine own undoing askest thou. Behold ! "
   And Brunhild looked, and saw, with down-crushed pride,
Forthdrawn from Chriemhild's robe of silken fold,
A ring she knew too well and zone of burnished gold.

LXII.

" These Siegfried won from thee and, laughing, gave
   To me ! " Then Brunhild spoke no word; too deep
The arrow smote; but yearnings for a grave
   Fell on her and an everlasting sleep;
   No more she sought her broken pride to keep,
But turned and passed among the whispering throng;
   Unheeding aught but pain, she swore to sweep

Siegfried from living men and brand her wrong
Deep in his widow's soul with burnings fierce and
    strong.

LXIII.

Now soon the city's myriad voices rose
    And buzzed the thing about, and soon the kings
The story heard. The door to endless woes
    In this King Gunther saw ; he felt the stings
    Of conscience, and remorse his baleful wings
About him flapped. And Siegfried heard with
    pain ;
    Straight to Chriemhild he went and heard what
        things
Had passed. Then his first wrath and last the
    chain
Of love between them wrenched with rough and
    angry strain.

LXIV.

But much the lady wept and much she clung
    About him that his wrath soon passed away ;
And he, forgiving, sighed that woman's tongue
    Such bitter coil should make; he mourned the
        day
    That he to Chriemhild gave the golden prey.
Then took they counsel how they might appease
    The kindled strife, Queen Brunhild's fury stay,
And Gunther hearten, who the bitter lees
Of shame and sorrow drank, with deep indignities.

LXV.

Lightly to Gunther Siegfried fared and spake
   Soft, healing things and bade him mend his cheer,
"Words are but words," he said, "and do not break
   Men's armour; women's strife we need not fear;
   These ladies have forgot themselves; a tear,
A smile, and all is well with them again.
   My wife is full of grief that she so near
The queen hath touched. To heal her sister's pain
She will do much; more swift is she to bless than bane."

LXVI.

Then Gunther, "That my sister is to blame
   I think not; Brunhild's pride this evil coil
Hath wound about us. No more love, but shame
   Shall I from Brunhild win. Methinks 't is toil
   Mis-spent this Valkyr's fury to assoyle;
Yet peace not war would I for mine and thine."
   Then Siegfried in his breast the healing oil
Of love poured, and, as one who drinks new wine,
King Gunther's soul revived, and he the fatal twine

LXVII.

That wrapped them all about in snaky fold,
   With careful hand to disentangle sought;
In other forms he tried the tale to mould
   Of by-gone days, and what his brother wrought

For him he hid in subtleties of thought.
This Brunhild sullen heard, all undeceived,
 Inly she gnawed her pain, but uttered nought
Or good or bad to Gunther. He believed
Her wrath at end; behind the veil he nought
 perceived.

LVIII.

Then the fair sister-queens met once again
 And Chriemhild gave good words and Brunhild
 smiled;
So smiles the frosty moon, when bud and grain
 In May she blasts; and Chriemhild, soon beguiled
 As guileless souls are, wept that she so mild
And sweet was, after words so deadly keen;
 And much she marvelled her own wrath so wild,
So bridleless, with sweet Brunhild had been;
In all men's ears she blest the quick-forgiving queen.

LXIX.

Thus there was hollow peace between the twain,
 And thus the kings the strife forgotten deemed;
That the spark even now the deadly train
 Of hate had fired, no soul about them dreamed,
 So fair and pleasant all things outward seemed
In that sweet summer time, so gaily sped
 The lordly jousts, so rich a sunlight streamed
On tower and town. Thus Siegfried ate his bread
With joy, nor saw the sword that shook above his
 head.

LAY THE SIXTH

THE LINDEN-LEAF

L

PRELUDE

The Linden-tree

O LINDEN-TREE, sweet linden-tree,
   All bathed in golden glow,
With thy branches swaying pleasantly
   In the charmed air to and fro ;

Drowsily hums thy murmurous dome
   With myriad airy wings,
Thy blossoms burst in golden foam
   The breeze to the sunbeam flings :

O linden-tree, how sweet to be
   Beneath thy branches laid,
With thy soft song lulling quietly,
   In the cool and scented shade ;

All day to gaze at the tremulous maze
   Then slip to balmy sleep,
When the flitting gleams of mystic dreams
   The senses spell-bound keep !

THE LINDEN-TREE

So burned of old thy leaves of gold
    Above the hunter's head,
When he sought repose at the long day's close
    On the mossed earth's quiet bed.

So drooped thy scented bloom above
    The Minnesinger's song,
Or the dance that sped with airy tread
    The summer evening long.

And once the stain of blood hath lain
    In thy still and sacred shade,
When a hero died for a woman's pride,
    By a brother's hand betrayed.

What soul-bewildering fumes arise
    From thy censer, slowly swung
By the priestly wind to evening skies,
    With vespers softly sung !

O linden fair, what magic rare
    Breathes down thy rustling shades !
Thy leaves unfold dim tales of old ;
    I hear the clash of blades :

Before me pass, as in a glass,
    Those Teuton warriors old ;
They rise and stand, as a living band,
    And not as a tale that 's told.

LAY THE SIXTH

The Linden=Leaf

I.

NOT long the fire-winged steeds had south-
ward turned,
Nor yet their glowing path its steep incline
Much shortened; still the festal torches burned
And still at Worms, in honour half divine,
Abode the hero, whose renown will shine
While German blood in German hearts shall beat,
Siegfried. The first small spark had fired the line,
Henceforth to blaze in fierce and deadly heat,
Till in one furnaced woe all agonies should meet,

II.

The Niblung woe. And yet the fatal strife,
By pride enkindled, waged seven morns ago,
By Chriemhild with her brother's haughty wife,
And her wrath-wakened words, that laid so low
Brunhilda's pride, for which ere long should flow
Such tears and blood, lay dark in memory,
Half-lost to her. And yet the kings of woe,
Dark-gathering, dreamed not, nor the foam could see
That tipped the up-gathered wave of imminent
destiny.

III.

As some fierce tigress of her cubs bereaved
　Rages, so Brunhild, to her bosom's core
Stabbed by her shame made public, raged and grieved;
　Adown her lustrous cheeks, like molten ore,
The hot tears poured; her anguish was too sore;
Von Troneck Hagen watched those teardrops falling,
　(A man more loyal never weapon bore),
He saw her grief, and on high Heaven calling,
To his liege queen he swore a vengeance heart-appalling.

IV.

This Hagen swore. And nights and morrows twain
　He brooded on it, held from any speech;
So broods red storm upon a breathless plain,
　So cling the vampire and the unsated leech;
　Then straitly he King Gunther did beseech
For vengeance on the man who wrought the woe
　To Brunhild. Thus was schemed the impious breach
Of faith, and planned the fratricidal blow;
And thus the smouldering sparks of hate began to glow.

V.

First, noise of war was made; then came a change,
　And all were bidden to a five days' chase,
Burgundians and Niblungs; and the range
　From Worms was distant one day's journeying space.

So Siegfried set himself with joyous face
To go a hunting, and it was the eve
  Of their departure; but with listless pace
Chriemhild, as one who newly learns to grieve,
Went, wrapt in boding fears she could not all
    believe;

VI.

For mystic dreams had thrilled her heart that night
  With portents, like to those in days gone by,
Ere her slim body gained its princely height,
  Or the full soul within her fired her eye;
  Now, as she walked upon the rampart high,
Dim-boding, Hagen marked her, and he came
  To bid her farewell; then with long-drawn sigh
She turned, and met the warrior's glance of flame
And told him all her dread, as with unchallenged
    claim

VII.

Upon his aid. "To whom in this distress
  For counsel can I turn, but thee, O friend?
Save thou my hero, and my soul shall bless
  Both thee and thine till time for me shall end."
  Then he his word most willingly doth lend:
And she, "When Siegfried slew the dragon fell,
  The guard of Niblung gold, he did unbend
His strained limbs in the brute's hot blood, and well
He bathed, and all his body sheathed in wound-
    proof shell.

VIII.

"But while my Siegfried bathed, an envious wind
    Stirred the sweet linden-tree that gave him shade,
And one light leaf came fluttering down behind
    The hero, and between his shoulders stayed,
So that one spot was vulnerable made;
What woe if spear or sword should smite him there!"
Then Hagen: "Noble queen, be undismayed:
The Niblung's life shall be my constant care,
But mark this spot upon the vesture he shall wear."

IX.

Then dews of joy suffused the lady's eyes,
    As, full of trust, she pressed the iron hand
Of Hagen, and she thanked him; passing wise
    She deemed the measure he so quickly planned;
    For who such deadly guile might understand?
And while her lord slept in the silent night,
    Herself unloosed from slumber's healing band,
She rose, to sew a cross of colour bright
Upon his garment laid to don with morning light.

X.

How the fierce heart in Hagen's bosom leapt
    When, on the morn he saw that fatal sign!
A little backward to the kings he stepped,
    And whispered it with darkly glowing eyne;
    But Gunther, like a reveller steeped in wine,

Shrank staggering, and his sister's farewell kiss
   Burnt his blanched cheek and made his eye-balls
      shine ;
Then mused he on his hard-won bridal bliss,
And Siegfried's generous aid and faith to him and
      his.

XI.

He mused on Brunhild's mien that fateful day
   What time the martial maid with sword and spear
Assailed him, and his soul shook with dismay,
   Knowing the fierce, unequal combat near
   With occult powers, mused how, with words of
      cheer,
Siegfried, in mystic robes of darkness veiled,
   Came, and while Gunther fighting would appear,
Over the war-maid's strength himself prevailed,
And with the beauteous bride and treasure home-
      wards sailed.

XII.

Then mused he on the golden zone and ring,
   Wrested by viewless hands in darkling fight.
Alas, that Siegfried should have breathed the thing
   To Chriemhild, and, alas, the fatal spite
   Of women, that all this had brought to light !
And then his cheek burnt hotter, as he thought
   That all lay open to his people's sight,
The binding and the shame Brunhilda wrought,
The aid more shameful still that Siegfried's prowess
      brought.

XIII.

But after she, unknowing, for his death
    Her lord had signed, Chriemhild in quiet lay,
Till slumber caught her softly-coming breath,
    And a grim vision rent the veil away
    From the dark future. Then in wild dismay
She screamed and woke, and in the dawning's chill
    Knelt white and trembling, and that he would stay
From hunting, prayed her lord with passioned will,
And told him all her dream and dread of coming
    ill.

XIV.

Then Siegfried, sleep-dazed, in the dusky light,
    With pitying love upon the fair queen gazed;
Touched by her terror and the pure delight
    Of beauty, in his arms he gently raised
    And soothed, like some young child with pain amazed,
The lady, gently chiding her weak fears;
" In vain," he said, " the occult powers blazed
Upon me in my boyhood's far-off years;
Why tremble now, when nought to hurt or harm
    appears?"

XV.

So, ere the first dews sparkled in the sun,
    Chriemhild with trembling touch her lord arrayed
For hunting; spear, bow, quiver, one by one,
    And lastly, Balmung, dread and mystic blade,

In flashing splendours in his baldric laid,
Then her white arms about her husband flung
  And wept, her lofty stature on him stayed;
And with strange agony the lips that clung
To his he kissed, nor knew what pain his bosom
    wrung.

XVI.

But Chriemhild knew that in that long last kiss,
  The bitterness of death lurked ; long gazed she
Upon the godlike form that bore her bliss
  Away; and thrice, with longing looks, to see
  Her face, he turned and paused, then, shaking free
The golden reins, spurred onward in the light ;
  A kingly sun with vassal stars was he,
Among those kings, of noble build and height ;
His face was very strong, with thought and beauty
    bright.

XVII.

Strange fires were tangled in his golden hair,
  Wild lightnings slumbered in his clear blue eye ;
Rich were his arms, his garb of fabric rare
  Blazed with the fatal cross in crimson dye.
  To gaze upon the hunters passing by
The burghers thronged about the city old,
  And, seeing Siegfried, raised an awe-struck cry—
" Lo ! he that won the Niblung's charmèd gold,
And slew the dragon-guard and scaled the rocky
    hold ! "

XVIII.

Then whispered they of Brunhild's ravished ring
  And girdle, and of service he had done,
Unspeakable, to the Burgundian king,
  And secretly the Valkyr's beauty won.
  This Hagen heard ; and that he had begun
He swore to finish ere that moon was high ;
  (So grew the darksome web the Norns had spun,)
And Gunther heard ; and while his brother's eye
Looked frankly to his own, moaned, shuddering,
    " He must die ! "

XIX.

Yet nothing of his purpose he let fall,
  But with the Niblung spoke in loving wise,
As they rode on by tower and steep-rooféd hall
  And balcony, alight with ladies' eyes,
  By quaint-carved storeys, climbing to the skies,
Dark-browed, and meeting like a woodland arch.
  Anon they lost the city's mingled cries,
And trod the silence made by pine and larch,
Then by the fortressed Rhine they bent their
    peaceful march.

XX.

By Siegfried's stirrup rode the younger kings,
  Gernot and Giselher, and they beguiled
The passing hours upon their lingering wings,
  With song and jest and tale with wonder piled ;

Anigh them moved the people, weird and wild,
Dark-faced and low of stature, from the land
  Of distant Niflheim ; dark amid the mild,
Bright-haired Burgundians gloomed that shadowy band,
Like troublous dreams that near the noon-day sleeper stand.

XXI.

All day they journeyed, till at vesper-time
  They rested by the river's still expanse ;
Afar they heard a convent faintly chime,
  They saw green shadows on the lit wave dance,
  And steep cliffs glowing in the sun's red glance ;
Around their simple fare the hunters lay,
  And told of heroes tried by battle's chance,
Of elves and shapes that shun the eye of day,
Until the marshalled stars formed up in calm array.

XXII.

Now when the wine leapt warmly in his veins,
  And earth lay steeped in solemn still repose,
Siegfried, not boding treason, loosed the reins
  Of free, confiding mirth, and spoke with those
  Around him of past things ; of mutual foes
And mutual friends, of far-off youthful days,
  When first they met in friendship's hallowed close,
Of Chriemhild and her beauty's far-spread praise ;
But Hagen noted all with fierce and hungry gaze.

XXIII.

And, seeing Siegfried gay beyond his use,
  Though he was never of a visage sad,
And so much moved that bright, rejoicing dews
  His vision dimmed at mention of the glad
  Past times, and Chriemhild and the little lad,
Their son, the fierce old warrior grimly mused
  On the dark saying that the gods make mad
The death-doomed; then the royal brothers used
Fair speech to Siegfried; thus was friendship's name abused.

XXIV.

All peaceful sped the slumber-breathing night,
  While squadroned stars wheeled by with noiseless tread,
And soon the pale east glimmered coldly white,
  Then flushed in awful glory rosy red;
  Up leapt the sun, his new-dipped splendours shed
On river, crag, and hill, and forest wide,
  The fresh earth flung the shadows from her head,
Her dewy face in fitful crimson dyed,
And all things deeply drank of life's returning tide.

XXV.

Then, one by one, beneath the firry spires
  And oaken domes, small, feathered minstrels sing,
Till a full chorus thrills the leafy choirs
  And hill and dale with joyous music ring,

Then, in his measure, every living thing
Swells the deep-hearted hymn of vital joy ;
　Hares gambol, squirrels frisk, on airy wing
Bees hum, and painted flies with sunbeams toy ;
And man, arising, fares abroad to his employ.

XXVI.

Far down beneath its cliffs the river lay,
　Beneath its towered cliffs, the storied Rhine,
And here it shunned the opening eye of day,
　And here, like sapphire, in the morning's shine
It sparkled ; now the rocks, incarnadine,
Transmute them silently to molten gold,
　And now the verdant slopes of blossomed vine
Flush gold beneath the rude precipitous hold,
Now the wide-beaming rays field, rock, and forest fold.

XXVII.

Forth fared the hunters with the opening dawn,
　Their quick steps brushed the dew-beads glittering white ;
They saw long sunrays smite the shimmering lawn,
　And golden lances pierce the forest night :
In woodcraft, as in all the arts of fight,
The kings excelled : before the welcome smoke
　Of breakfast fires upcurled, in many a flight
Winged arrows from their humming bow-strings broke,
And many a wild life bled in glades of beech and oak.

XXVIII.

In his hot fury fell a tuskèd boar,
   Yet, dying, held both men and hounds at bay;
And Gunther he had silenced evermore,
   Him charging, where he could not break away
   For brush; but Siegfried saw the king's dismay,
And, leaping on the beast, with ready steel
   He slew him. Then, with darkened brow, a prey
To anguish, Gunther turned upon his heel
And mused on Siegfried's faith to him in woe and weal.

XXIX.

But never swerved the fire of Hagen's gaze
   From the doomed hero; with a ceaseless care
He watched him secretly in all his ways,
   (So the keen hunter watches from his lair
   The lion, all unconscious of the snare),
That he might smite him where the fatal cross
   Gave entrance to the weapon of the slayer:
But the prince moved so swiftly, all to loss
His pains turned, and in rage he trampled mire and moss,

XXX.

Wrath-brooding. Little sport was his that day
   So strongly was the hunter's instinct bent
On tracking to his death a nobler prey;
   And evermore before his vision went
   The weeping face of Brunhild, and it lent
New fury to the fire that in him glowed.
   So fared they till the sun's first heat was spent,

And the bright fire-maned coursers swiftly trode
The blue to burning gold adown the westward road.

XXXI.

Sun-spent and weary were the hunters then,
　And fain were they to rest and fain to drink;
But the great drouth had stilled in wood and glen
　The song of rills and made all rivers shrink,
　When Gunther suddenly a missing link
Of memory captured, and he spoke of trees,
　Soft-glooming by a bubbling fountain's brink;
And Hagen saw them darkening in the breeze,
And thither sped while still the princes lay at ease.

XXXII.

Then Siegfried, all unconscious of his doom,
　Humoured the young kings in such boyish play
As strong men love, a foot-race to the bloom
　Of limes, beneath whose shade the waters lay.
　So the three kings their weapons cast away
For lightness, but the Dragon-slayer kept,
　With reckless ease of strength, his whole array,
And over bending fern he glanced and swept
And reached the spring, while far behind the tired
　　kings stepped.

XXXIII.

A living spring gushed in the dim, sweet shade,
　With cool, deep moss and drooping fern o'ergrown;
By day, by night, the escaping waters made
　A pleasant music on the rugged stone;

M

Three sister-linden's arms, together thrown
Athwart the bright wave, kept the sun aloof;
   All day in soft and drowsy undertone
Winged people murmured in the gold-green roof,
And pale lights trembled through its closely-braided
      woof.

XXXIV.

A moment bent the form of hero mould
   Above its image in the diamond well,
Then eagerly within the water cold
   The Niblung plunged his hand, a hollow shell,
   And raised it full but drank not; for it fell
Upon him to await in knightly guise
   The coming of the kings; thus, old books tell,
Did the high breeding of those times advise;
So, thirsting still, he stood close watched by hostile
      eyes.

XXXV.

Then, leisurely, as one who moves at ease
   In his own hall, unvexed by any care,
He leant his goodly spear against the trees,
   Unclasped his tunic, made his hot brow bare,
   Breathing with joy the cool, spray-freshened air,
Laid by all weapons, even the charmèd blade,
   The elf-forged Balmung, and defenceless there
He stood, untroubled, in the linden shade,
Nor dreamed his courteous deed with murder would
      be paid.

XXXVI.

Him Hagen marked, and in his bloodshot eye
  The lurid flame of vengeance fiercer glowed.
Then, hot and panting, full of jollity,
  The brothers came, and Gunther slowly strode
  Behind them ; as a tired man drops a load
He dropped his body by the water's brink,
  And Siegfried, also bending, turned and showed
The fatal cross, and scooped the cool, bright drink
With curving palm ; then quick, before the stirred wave's wink,

XXXVII.

Leapt Hagen panther-like upon the spear,
  Grasped it and kept it in his rough, right hand,
And with the other caught the quiver near
  And bow, and even the Niblung's shining brand,
  The sacred Balmung, in its jewelled band,
He seized and hurled in flashing wheels away ;
  And, ere the doomed man guessed the treason planned
Or deemed himself in turn the hunter's prey,
His own spear through the cross had made its fated way.

XXXVIII.

Then, with a dread and far-resounding cry,
  Death-stricken, Siegfried sprang upon his feet,
When, turning in his mortal agony,
  His eyes the flaming orbs of Hagen meet,

Intent to make the deadly deed complete;
Transfixed by his own spear and paling fast,
  The prince with aimless strokes the void air beat,
And all his deeds in one swift moment passed
Before his fading eyes, with blinding death-film
    glassed.

XXXIX.

But, ere he died, the loyal, generous soul
  In one word, "Traitor!" from his wan lips burst;
And suddenly he felt the darkness roll
  Away from past things, and he saw the worst,
  The treason that had plotted from the first
Against him. But he did not tamely die.
  Vainly he sought his arms; the hand accursed
Had moved them; but he saw beside him lie
His shield, and smote with that the murderers
    pressing nigh.

XL.

Thus, bleeding from a brother's treacherous hand,
  The princely stag the fierce hounds held at bay;
They did not scorn to strike, that coward band,
  To strike the stricken and defenceless prey;
  But only by the lime-leaf's fatal way
The prince was vulnerable; so in vain
  They sought the charm-bound Dragon-slayer to
    slay;
While he in noble fury smote amain
Till the woods rang and cleft was Hagen's casque
    in twain,

XLI.

And many a warrior fell, such deadly might
  Yet lived within the wounded hero's arm,
Although the shadows of death's imminent night
  Had darkened all his being's fateful charm.
  At last he fell, but his great soul and warm
Not easily might leave its palace fair,
  He fell, and nearer closed the murderous swarm;
His blood dyed all the wood-flowers blooming there,
And Gunther's glances pale he sought with eyes of prayer.

XLII.

Then, "O my brother!" cried the dying man,
  With gasping breath and slowly-darkening eyes,
While drops of anguish from his pale brow ran,
  "Speak once more brotherly before I die,
  And swear to me by all thou holdest high
And holy to protect thy father's child,
  The desolate Chriemhild, lest my blood should cry
To Heaven on thy knightly faith defiled,—
Guest, brother, liegeman, friend, by treason foul beguiled.

XLIII.

"I charge thee by the love of olden days
  My orphaned son and widowed wife defend;
If ever thou wouldst walk in pleasant ways,
  If ever thou wouldst call a good man friend;

And Heaven to thee and thine for ever send
All blessing ! For thy blood lives in their veins,
  To thee and Chriemhild did the same lives lend
Their life. Speak out before my faint lamp wanes,
Speak out, and cleanse thy soul from treason's
      shameful stains.

XLIV.

"Ay me ! my little lad, that men should say,
  That men should say of Chriemhild's princely son,
'His own blood did his father's life betray,
  By brother's hands his father was undone.'
  But lest thy love to bitterness should run,
Seeing in my son the features of his sire,
  And thou shouldst visit on this helpless one
Dark memories his sweet eyes might inspire,
Come near and clasp my hand and let thy wrath
      expire.

XLV.

"For ever blotted out be this dark day
  From thy remembrance ! Only think of me
As of the brother of thy heart, thy stay
  When need was sorest, one who trusted thee
  To death, and, dying, turned to thee to see
His best friend—yet the thing is very hard,
  To fall so meanly—and by treachery—
Not as a warrior dies, face foremost, scarred
By battle's burning joy, in sight of fame's award.

XLVI.

"Alas my Chriemhild ! for her gentle sake
 I would my tide of life might turn again :
Not death I fear ; the warrior must take
 Battle's grim odds upon the bloody plain ;
 But to die thus, unshriven, with foul stain
Of fresh-done trespass. Yet, thro' my soul's war
 A soft voice breathes, 'Thou hast not lived in
  vain.'
And, spite of all my sin, perchance, afar,
I may behold God's light from some sweet-shining
  star.

XLVII.

" For I repent me. Pray now for my soul,
 Fair brother, and let holy rites be done
For this spent body, when the life-tides roll
 No more in it for ever ; do not shun
 My memory." He ceased ; for now, out-spun
Was his thin thread of life. And Gunther, bowed
 To earth by shame and sorrow, lay as one
Death-stricken, and for anguish wept aloud,
All wept, and none refrained but Hagen in that
  crowd.

XLVIII.

Now Hagen had been wounded in the strife,
 Sore wounded, and his casque was cleft in twain,
And when he pierced the prince, the unprisoned life
 Gushed out and sprinkled him with ruddy rain,

His own blood mingled with that shameful stain
Upon his raiment : he, with passion torn,
   Flouted the dying hero ; "Not again
Through thee our queen shall sorrow; but, forlorn
And widowed, thy proud dame shall weep from
      night till morn.

XLIX.

"And none shall comfort her. And thy young whelp
   Shall howl beneath a stranger's pitiless blow,
And he shall cry, and cry in vain, for help,
   While thou with all thy strength art lying low ;
I do rejoice me that I wrought thee woe."
Thus the betrayer with fierce flaming eyes,
   Staunching his blood that never ceased to flow ;
But Gunther pardon craved with heart-wrung sighs,
And all around him wept as when a father dies.

L.

Then darkened all the sweet and sylvan scene,
   The green earth heaved the closing eyes before,
And all things were as they had never been,
   While the last death-pangs Siegfried's body tore;
   But when his spirit passed, his lips once more,
With Chriemhild's name moved, and his strong
      heart broke,
   The stalwart limbs stretched stiffening in gore ;
Like evening's sunbeam, the last words he spoke
Unearthly loveliness in his pale face awoke.

LI.

Majestic, like a lofty god at rest,
  He lay upon his mossy woodland bed;
Some golden blossoms fluttered to his breast,
  And thick-leaved boughs encanopied his head;
  But the cool, warbling wave was stained with red,
Red was the balmy woodruff on the ground,
  On all his garments and his gear were spread
Red blood-drops, and his lofty brow was bound
With the dread damps and chills of death's
  unbreaking swound.

LII.

But awe and shuddering seized the brothers twain,
  Gernot and Giselher; bewildered sore,
Scarce wist they how it chanced the guest was slain;
  And who began and who the life-thread shore,
  They questioned; and the Niblungs stood before
Their dead, and asked what chance this sorrow
  wrought.
  Then Gunther spoke of evil hap that bore
Him deathwards. But the undreading Hagen raught
Towards the spear and cried: "This vengeance
  to him brought,

LIII.

"And this hand smote him, and not easily
  Will he arise to work us woe again.
Who shall avenge him? Not the few we see,
  Faint-hearted Niblungs, who are in his train."

Then the young brothers: " There has fallen a
    stain
Upon us that no blood can wash away,
  Not though the heavens should break in gory rain,
And quenched in blood were the great eye of day,
And one day our doomed race in blood this deed
    will pay."

LIV.

And then they raised upon a shield of gold
  The lifeless form and bore it silently,
On cross-laid spears in Siegfried's banner rolled,
  Beneath the changing arch of sky and tree;
  The Niblungs, Burgunds, and the brothers three
In silence followed; but who wrought the woe,
  Von Troneck Hagen, laughed in bitter glee;
And when the evening star had fallen low
And every household fire in Worms long ceased to
    glow,

LV.

They reached the city and so stilly passed,
  That no man of their home-returning deemed.
Then the dead warrior, with face aghast
    And wan, without the house where Chriemhild
        dreamed,
    They laid and left. The pale, pure starlight
        beamed
Sadly, and waned in mist; the watchful cock
  Gave warning ere the first white dawning gleamed,

What time day's cares at sleep-barred spirits knock,
And, at Aurora's touch, morn's pearly gates unlock.

LVI.

Then the deep minster bells began to chime
    For mass, and to the holy house of prayer
Went Lady Chriemhild in the dawning time,
    And men before her flaming torches bare,
    When, on the pavement in the ruddy glare,
They caught the glitter of a shield of gold,
    And through dense mist the warrior lying there,
Scarce saw they, ere a sudden shrill cry told
Their lady saw and knew that form's heroic mould.

LVII.

Ah! who may paint the deadly agony
    Of Chriemhild, when she clasped the silent dead,
Kissed the sealed eyes that never more would see,
    Cradled upon her breast the helpless head,
    Washed with hot tears the stains of dull dark red,
And, for warm kisses, felt the icy chill
    Of lips whence love and life were ever fled,
Of pulses, once so strong, for ever still,
Till in a death-like swoon she lost all sense of ill?

LVIII.

Even the rough linksmen stood aside in awe,
    Heart-stricken by the lady's utter woe,
And when her swoon of agony they saw,
    Some tears from one man's eyes began to flow,

The other groaned and turned his torch, that so
It might not fall upon the piteous scene ;
Then from the hall ran serving-folk to know
What that dread cry in the dim dawn should mean,
With Sigmund, Siegfried's sire, and his bereavèd
    queen.

LIX.

Now, at the mother's heart-struck cry, the life
    Came pulsing through the widow's breast again,
Back, like the cutting of a keen-edged knife,
    Flashed the full consciousness of bitter pain,
    And Chriemhild rose, and looked upon the slain,
Her wide eyes all amazed with agony ;
    She marked him weaponless, and tracked the
        stain
Of life-blood to the silken cross, that she
Herself had sewn, in trust of Hagen's loyalty.

LX.

Then all the lovely lustre of her eyes
    Was altered, and the deathless fire of hate
Changed all her features and her gentle guise
    Of speech, and marred the sweet and tender state
    Of womanhood upon her, till the great,
Fierce tide of anguish burst, and thus she spake :
    " Thy spirit passed not through the glorious gate
Of battle, nor did foe thine armour break
With sword cuts ; but thy death crept on thee like
        a snake,

LXI.

"In treachery from behind." Then Siegfried's sire
  This hearing, bent, hand-shadowed, in the light
That flickered red in gusts of smoke and fire.
  He saw, and knew that she had read aright
  The dreadful riddle of that tragic sight;
And Siegfried's mother wept that she had borne
  A son so noble for so sad a plight;
And Chriemhild stood of joy for ever lorn,
And with a gust of rain awoke the wan-eyed morn.

LXII.

Then, with the pale day, all the city came
  With lamentation wild, and awe-struck woe,
And many armed them to avenge the shame
  Of the strong Dragon-slayer, lying low
  In blood; but no man wist who dealt the blow.
And Sigmund would have taken arms, despite
  His weight of years, to smite the unknown foe,
But Chriemhild clung to him; her lips were white,
She held him with the terror of her glances bright.

LXIII.

"Not yet awhile, not yet awhile," she cried,
  "The fated hour of vengeance is not yet!"
So he stood awed and musing, at her side,
  Noting her rigid face and eyes unwet;

Then they took up the murdered prince and set
With reverence upon a seemly bed,
   In a fit room, where priest and warrior met
To pray and watch in turn beside the dead,
And tapers through the gloom a spectral radiance
      shed.

LXIV.

Where, like the work of some great sculptor's hand,
   In pure, cold marble, and exceeding fair,
But terrible, so that men gazing, stand
   And cross themselves with murmured, hasty prayer,
   Knelt Chriemhild in the wan and waxen glare,
With all the azure brilliance of her eyes
   Concentred in the mute face, unaware
Of aught, while men filed by to recognize,
Before it sank to dust, the hero's mortal guise.

LXV.

But Chriemhild waited, speechless all the day,
   Unmoving, till the night wrought thicker gloom,
Till the tall tapers shed a purer ray,
   And Gunther paced with Brunhild thro' the room,
   While music wailed the hero's timeless doom ;
Then Chriemhild rose, while bitter, burning scorn
   Blazed in her eyes and scorched her beauty's
      bloom,
Crying, "Go, murderer ! feign not to mourn,
Nor vaunt unblushing here thy kingly faith forsworn"!

LXVI.

Then Gunther turned, shame-smitten. But his queen
  Exulting, mocked the desolate woman's woe,
And cried, "Ha, ha! Was Balmung's edge so keen?
  And sped the shaft so truly from the bow?
  Struck in the back, too, turned to flee his foe!"
But Chriemhild spoke no word and made no sign,
  Only her eyes burnt into Brunhild's so
The Valkyr quailed and went; then in the shine
Of tapers Chriemhild watched the slayer to divine.

LXVII.

And when the second morning fired the east,
  Paling the tapers in the chamber drear,
Where the wan Chriemhild's watch had never ceased,
  Von Troneck Hagen came to Siegfried's bier;
  And suddenly, when the slayer's step drew near,
The icy blood in crimson witness burst
  From Siegfried's heart, transfixed with his own spear.
Then Chriemhild rose, with wild eyes all athirst
For vengeance, and in thrilling voice the traitor cursed.

LXVIII.

Within the vaulted minster, where began
  The fatal strife for which such blood should flow,
They laid the body of the kingly man;
  Then the three brother-sovereigns strove to show,

By fit observances and pomp of woe,
Sorrow and honour for a brother slain;
Long ranks of mailèd warriors followed slow
To mournful dirges in the funeral train,
And all the city folk with mourning filled the fane.

LXIX.

There in the minster's still and solemn gloom,
  With blazonry and storied panels dight,
In carven marbles fair, a splendid tomb
  Was planned for him. But ere the grave's long night
Shrouded the dreadless hero from her sight
Chriemhild unveiled the well-known, well-loved face,
  So awful in its frozen beauty's light,
Kissed the cold lips and clasped the body's grace,
Then stood alone and vowed the death of all her race.

LXX.

Now when the tomb closed over Siegfried's form,
  A strong, swift shudder shook the hearts of men,
Above the city lowered in gathering storm
  A black, low muttering thunder-cloud, and then
  Thick mist rolled up on winds that swept a fen
Till all the city sheeted stood in gloom,
  Where wild shapes moved and shrieked and shrieked again;
Then pallor sat on cheeks of richest bloom
And every soul the shadow felt of imminent doom.

www.ingramcontent.com/pod-product-compliance
Lightning Source LLC
Chambersburg PA
CBHW020053200426
43197CB00050B/608